Practical Artificial Intelligence
An Enterprise Playbook

Practical Artificial Intelligence

An Enterprise Playbook

Alan Pelz-Sharpe & Kashyap Kompella

Deep Publishing

Design: Ellen Zhao, BURO-GDS

Printed in the United States of America
First Printing, 2019

Deep Publishing
200 Innovative Way
Nashua, NH 03062

ISBN 9781686799853

Table of Contents

Acknowledgements

It turns out that writing a short book on a big topic is hard, really hard. In fact, it would have been impossible without so much help, and so many thanks are due. Firstly, for the support and love of my wife Sandra, who by regularly asking 'How is the book coming along?" kept it actually coming along. Writing with my friend, AI expert, mentor and support Kashyap was a privilege and one I will long cherish. Together I believe we have crafted something that can make a positive difference.

Thanks also to the awesome, editing skills of both Graham Southorn and Fiona my daughter who provided painful, but invaluable feedback throughout the process. Ellen, who may actually be the world's best designer, as she made everything look beautiful in a way that only she can. And finally, a special thanks to Peggy and the AIIM team who gave us the opportunity to build the AI training course that originally inspired the book.

– Alan

Encore! My debt of gratitude to all the wonderful folk Alan mentions above. And, thank you, Alan, for being so much fun to collaborate with, not only on this book but also on several projects during the last 15 years I've known you.

It really takes a family for a book to see the light, and special thanks to my sunshine, Divya.

Finally, dear reader, a big thank you! If you find this book useful, please share it with your friends.

– Kashyap

Introduction

Artificial Intelligence is huge news. Not a day passes without discussions on the impact of AI on the workplace in the press. However, here's the reality: most AI projects today don't work well at all. The world is full of failed AI projects.

We believe that AI has great promise to bring about radical improvements in the workplace and industry at large; the technology is sound, the math behind it robust. The market is enthusiastic and billions of dollars a year are being invested in AI; billions more will be spent over the coming years. Nevertheless, AI projects often never get off the ground, fail early, or disappoint in the long run. So we decided to ask: why?

We got our chance to explore the reasons in depth when we were commissioned by AIIM (Association of Intelligent Information Management) to design a practical training course for AI. Our work involved speaking to many organizations around the world regarding their experiences with AI. We talked to public and private sector firms, AI technology firms, developers, consultants, and implementers of AI. A pattern quickly emerged as to why AI projects were so problematic. We were able to capture and analyze these insights to share them with you in both the training course and in this book.

However, more importantly, we have codified how to implement AI correctly and dramatically improve your chances of success. The truth of the matter is that the reasons for past failures, though multiple, were possible to codify and remedy. The remedy does not require advanced mathematical skills or deep insights into the world of coding and application development. The remedy is a practical and methodical playbook for AI best practices.

In our research, we found major consulting firms and small in-house project teams trying to apply traditional approaches for IT project development to AI. To summarize, the reason that past projects have been so problematic is that AI projects are very different to traditional IT projects.

In this book, we show you how to approach your AI project from beginning to end correctly. We provide you with a practical playbook to use in your work, one that takes you from an initial strategy, through to a successful deployment to deliver transformative results. We also provide you with an unbiased and truly independent perspective on AI, exploring its strengths and its weaknesses, where it should and should not be used, and even going so far as to prime you on the "dark side" of AI. There is no doubt that AI provides great power to change the way you work, but as Uncle Ben of Spiderman fame advised us, "With great power comes great responsibility." AI can go wrong, and when it does, it can have devastating consequences. The guidance we provide you here helps you to avoid those situations and leads you to success.

In our regular work at Deep Analysis and rpa2ai Research, we provide advice, guidance, and research into the use of AI in enterprise. Over the years we have connected and worked with many organizations, both public and private, ranging from the food supply chain to law firms. In some cases, our clients want to get familiar with the concepts of AI as their company has expressed a desire to leverage AI technologies. In other cases, our work focuses on helping firms to select the right AI technologies. In yet others, we work to unravel and explain what went wrong with the firm's failed AI project. However, it is always a two-way street. We learn from our clients about their real-world experiences and expectations of AI systems.

For example, we have engaged with many financial services and insurance firms that are exploring and, in many cases, already using AI in some parts of their business. Many financial services firms already use AI to examine claims and trades, to detect suspicious patterns and flag them quickly. Sometimes this fraud detection work is pretty basic, looking for known patterns of fraudulent activities. Sometimes it is more sophisticated, crawling through claimants' social media accounts and online presence activities. Insurance claims have long been plagued by sometimes clumsy, but often quite sophisticated fraudulent activities. The use of AI holds much promise to reduce the number of fraudulent claims and to detect fraudulent claims quickly before pushing them further through the claims process.

Similarly, we have seen law firms become early adopters of AI. The legal sector has had a (justified) reputation for lagging behind other sectors to embrace new technologies. AI is rapidly changing that. In the legal sphere, the typical driver for the use of AI is a bit different from insurance. In the legal world, the sheer volume and complexity of the legal documentation cases makes AI an ideal technology to automate many manual, costly, error-ridden, and overwhelming tasks and activities.

Insurance and law are traditional document-and-file-rich sectors that are ideal for AI, but AI is reaching into many other sectors, such as hospitality. Hotels are now installing Amazon Alexa in guest rooms to automate customer service activities like ordering room service or checking out. AI is in use in agriculture, manufacturing, healthcare, and art. A truly interconnected and intelligent digital world is in development. The beauty of this is that what is learned in one sector can often be shared in another. As we often like to say: in AI, it's all data. The use of AI in manufacturing brings us process efficiencies; in agriculture and food, the traceability of products; in healthcare, a vital interest in accuracy and privacy; and in art, the importance of provenance.

Many existing and well-explored use cases for AI can feed into your specific requirements. What are others doing that I can replicate (or avoid doing), regardless of whether they are in my industry or not? You should have as broad an awareness of the possibilities open to you as possible and learn from how others have fared. AI has no interest in the existing boundaries of business; it considers everything to be data. That's a significant shift in how technology was used in the past, and how we have learned from one another in our deployments of IT services and applications.

For example, if you are a traditional document and process-centric company looking to use AI, don't limit your vision to what has worked in the past but could be improved. We recently engaged with a seemingly traditional, old-school company that wants to use AI not just to automate its paperwork-dense operating environment, but to add voice and gestures as a means to interface with its operations, ideas, and approaches taken from consumer technologies. AI enables you to rethink the way that you work. Of course, rethinking and imagining are one thing, while actually making the desired changes are another thing altogether; but the building blocks of AI are standard and not as complicated or daunting as many imagine.

So, no matter where you are on your AI journey, this book is for you. Everything we share here is drawn from real-world project successes and failures. Sadly, we have seen too many failures that had the potential to be very successful. They failed because they selected the wrong tools, took the wrong strategic approach, were unaware of what others have already done, and didn't know how AI projects differ from traditional IT projects. This book has been written to help you to be successful and to learn from others that have already taken some journeys down the AI road; our goal is to help you move forward and to avoid trying to reinvent the wheel. Trust us; we see lots of people reinventing the wheel, selecting the wrong tools, structuring their projects incorrectly, and choosing to deploy AI in situations where it should not be utilized.

In this book, we'll be covering everything you need to know about devising your AI strategy, which tools to buy, how to run an AI project, including how to select a project team, as well as exploring the pitfalls and AI biases you need to be aware of. It's a handy primer drawn from our own and our clients' experiences of using AI in the enterprise.

Enjoy the book, use it responsibly, and tell us about your experiences and share your feedback as you progress along your AI journey. We are on the journey with you, and together we can make this work!

1

AI is Everywhere

So, the first questions are... when, where, and how can you apply AI? There are clearly many different areas that AI can be applied: everything from self-driving cars to robotics, from medical diagnosis to drug discovery. We commonly see AI applied through the use of digital assistants and chat bots. We see AI in systems that make recommendations or that analyze sentiment. However, this book also focuses on the more mundane (but no less critical) use cases that are common in every organization: back and front office content and process operations.

Think of it this way: with AI we can predict demand, identify patterns and draw insights from documents, deliver dynamic pricing, segment our customers, and cross- or up-sell to them. In a sense, AI is everywhere; it can be used to both protect and attack our infrastructure. As such, we can easily imagine that AI is a good fit for any business situation. But it's more complex than that—some AI methods are good for some things and not so good for others. Sometimes AI is not a fit at all. We need to carefully select the situations in which we leverage AI, where we apply it to improve or even automate an existing activity. To make sense of this, and to start our AI journey, we need to break AI down into digestible chunks. Let's start with two big chunks: predictive versus exploratory AI.

➡ Types of AI Applications

The different types and uses of AI are seemingly endless, but broadly speaking, there are two main categories where we can apply AI. There are *predictive* use cases and *exploratory* use cases. Let us look at each of them in turn to understand why these two categories are so fundamental and important to understand. This is the starting point to making sense of how and where to use AI.

➡ Predictive AI

With *predictive* AI, we are trying to *predict* a business metric or *predict* what action a customer might take. For example, in retail we may want to predict what product a customer might buy. In an insurance claim processing office, we may want to predict when an insurance claim might occur. If you stop to think for a moment or two, you will likely come up with many use cases where in essence, we want to make accurate predictions.

On the other hand, with *exploratory AI*, we are looking to determine the underlying patterns or groups in data. We might do this to understand how customers are segmented, or to use another finance example, to explore what specific factors contribute to loan defaults.

Predictive and exploratory are two fundamentally different approaches. Once you know where your AI ambitions lie, deciding whether the work is predictive or exploratory in nature will be the typical starting point for your AI project.

You may have grand ambitions to transform your organization with AI, or you may just want to play around and experiment with AI in one small area. Either way, once you have identified an area of interest to apply AI to, always ask yourself whether this is an exploratory or a predictive use case. Depending on which one it is, you will approach the project quite differently and use different AI tools, models, and approaches. Let us take a couple of real world examples here to illustrate the difference between predictive and exploratory AI.

➜ Exploratory AI

At the core of most businesses are documents, whether they take the form of invoices, statements and purchase orders, or contracts, patient files or reports. Documents are the lifeblood of business. AI is already being used to sort and categorize documents more quickly and more accurately than was ever possible before. The sheer volume and richness of the data stored and gathered by document management systems make it an ideal target for exploratory AI use cases that can bring fast and measurable business value. The focus here is to find patterns, classifications, and groups, to sort and categorize using AI to automate that work.

➜ Predictive AI

The world of web content management and online digital marketing has been quick off the mark in the use of predictive AI. It is already used extensively to make predictive content recommendations. Predictive AI is also used to improve the quality of search results and result ranking. AI is also used extensively to predict the best times and locations to automatically place adverts online. Often the goal is to predict customer behavior, to make the right recommendations, to display the right adverts to guide them to the right purchase point or product. Predictive AI is something we encounter every day. That also means that we are all aware of its limitations: spam is not always correctly identified, search results can be frustrating, and adverts can be distracting and way off the mark. Impressive though the technology is, it is an early indication that AI is not magic.

→ Prescriptive AI

There is another species of AI that we have not yet mentioned called prescriptive AI. It can be thought of as an extension of predictive AI. Prescriptive AI technology tells us what we should do if certain things happen in the future. This kind of AI uses simulation algorithms to advise on potential outcomes and to answer the basic question: "What should we do?"

This is the easiest way to think of the two kinds of AI: *exploratory* gives us insights into the past. We can look at what has gone before, spot patterns and associations to sort and manage.

Predictive AI forecasts and tells us what could or likely will happen in the future. Prescriptive AI simulates possible future outcomes and gives us answers and advises us on what actions we should take.

Knowing where your AI project best fits is an important starting point. Defining this will help you to choose the right AI options and set realistic expectations regarding future outcomes and the value your project can bring. The key takeaway here is that AI can be used to explore and describe what you already have, in ways or at a speed that a human could not. AI can look at patterns of behavior and predict what future outcomes will be. Finally, AI can provide guidance on how you should respond to events based on its analysis of the possible outcomes.

➡ The Foundations of AI

Let's demystify this technology called AI. First, understand that the term AI is a catch-all term for a lot of different technological approaches and tools. Having a basic understanding of the key differences will help you to select the right AI approaches for your project and understand its limitations. In writing this section we have assumed that you have no prior knowledge of AI, that you are not a professional data scientist, and that you have little-to-no interest in the core mathematics behind the AI technologies! Even though we are going to describe the technologies at a layman level, we will explain the key differences between traditional IT and AI. Once you have read this, there is a decent chance you will be the most informed person in the room. AI is too often shrouded in unnecessary mystery, so here we play the role of AI myth busters.

The first myth to bust is that most AI is not really AI at all. Artificial Intelligence sounds more impressive than Machine Learning, but almost every AI-labelled product you will encounter is really a Machine Learning product at heart. Most organizations that believe they are using AI are actually using Machine Learning. So, what is the difference between the two?

➡ What is Machine Learning?

Machine Learning is an approach that allows computer programs to automatically improve through experience. The more they learn, the better they get. In essence, Machine Learning tools will look at a large set of documents (for example), spot patterns in those documents, and label them. An example would be: this is what an invoice looks like, this is an address field, this is a purchase order number, this is the quantity of products shipped, etc. When the Machine Learning tool looks at a new set of documents, it will apply the knowledge from the previous learning set and automatically identify the invoices and purchase order numbers, etc. There is a bit more to it than that, but for now that's what you need to know about Machine Learning.

➡ What is Artificial Intelligence?

Artificial Intelligence, on the other hand, is technology that behaves in ways that previously required human intelligence. To put it another way, true AI tools can sense, reason, act, and adapt to situations. AI is beyond Machine Learning, yet it needs Machine Learning to understand and optimize the decisions it makes. AI uses the learnings of Machine Learning to simulate actual intelligence.

Confusing? Don't worry; in principle, it doesn't matter much. What matters is that you understand that what you are being sold is often overhyped and not quite as smart as the sellers would lead you to believe. That being said, the right tool in the right situation can make dramatic changes to your business. You may have noticed that in this book we tend to use the term AI as a general term, as everyone else does today. But for the purists and the technology buyers that want to put the sellers on the back foot in any sales discussions, asking "How is this really AI?" can tell sellers that they shouldn't mess with you. It's a smart question to ask, and they will likely have to answer "Well no, it's really just ML." That's a great starting point for due diligence from a buyer's point of view!

Most of the time, the AI you will use in your organizations will most likely be Machine Learning tools. But even if not as sophisticated as an AI system that tries to mimic true human activities, they do still need to be approached fundamentally differently from the use of traditional IT programming. Machine Learning requires a mind shift.

→ Traditional Programming versus ML

In traditional programming, things are logical and pretty simple. You define some rules, you input some data, and you get an output in the form of a decision.

Machine learning and AI take a very different approach. Machine learning takes past data and outcomes as its starting point. It then automatically infers rules and conditions based on its analysis of the past data and outcomes. Those rules are applied to any new input data to drive outcomes and decisions. In simple terms, machine learning learns from the past and applies its analysis to new data to drive future outcomes. In the next section, we will look at four types of Machine Learning: Supervised, Semi-Supervised, Unsupervised and Reinforcement Learning.

→ Types of Machine Learning

Oftentimes, machine learning will need to be supervised; it will have human input to ensure that data is labeled correctly and that it remains focused on the goals and outcomes you desire.

Similarly, you might want to reinforce the machine learning system by providing it with feedback–rewarding it when it gives correct results and providing it with constructive feedback when it makes an error.

There are times, though, when you will not supervise the machine learning system at all: for example, when you don't really have any idea of the correct answer or there is no specific initial focus for its machinations. You may want to show it a pile of customer data and ask it to identify hidden buyer groups, finding correlations among buying trends that would not be feasible to undertake manually.

→ Supervised Learning

Supervised learning uses a predictive algorithm that uses training data and feedback from humans to learn the relationship between given inputs to a given output. For example, is this a duck?

We show the system pictures of ducks, and pictures of other birds and animals that are not ducks so that it learns to know the difference. Once it has been through that process, it knows when a picture is of a duck, or when it is not a duck.

How exactly do we do that? We label every column of input data and define the output variable. We train the system on this data, and once it becomes reasonably accurate at identifying the ducks in the data we gave it (data where we knew this was definitely a duck and this was not a duck), we then let it loose on new data to do the classification automatically for us.

We use supervised learning when we know how to classify the input data (we know what a duck looks like) and we know what we want to predict, ducks from a mass of non-duck like imagery.

Beyond the world of ducks and other aquatic animals, we see supervised learning used in areas such as sales to understand marketing spend, sales channels, and prices that are charged by our competitors. We may also get a little cleverer and predict customer churn, how long a customer is likely to stay with us, predicting that from analysis of past customer loyalty patterns. The bottom line here is that we know what we are looking for and we can supervise the system to learn to look for the same things.

→ Unsupervised Learning

The opposite of supervised learning is by definition unsupervised learning. Here, we are not trying to predict a variable. Instead, we want to discover hidden patterns to identify groups or clusters in the data. In unsupervised learning, we allow the algorithm to analyze all the input data by itself. We don't give it a specific output variable (eg. this is a duck). We allow it to create its own classifications. For example, it may identify things that are similar to one another (birds), and automatically recognize that rabbits and hedgehogs look different to birds.

In unsupervised learning situations we give the algorithm unlabeled data. We allow it to infer structures itself from the data we provide it, and in turn, we allow it to group data into categories that display similarities.

We use unsupervised methods when we ourselves don't know how to classify data. We want the algorithm to identify hidden patterns and do the classification of these groups for us.

We use this approach for situations such as segmenting customers or providing recommendations to customers based on the past preferences of similar customers.

→ Semi-Supervised Learning

Semi-supervised, as you may likely guess, falls somewhere between supervised and unsupervised learning. Semi-supervised learning uses a small amount of labeled data (we know what we are looking for) along with a typically much larger amount of unlabeled data.

By using some labeled data, we basically give the system a head start, a cheat sheet of sorts, that hopefully guides the algorithm to provide more meaningful and relevant models and outcomes.

When would we use this approach? Typically, we would use semi-supervised learning in situations where it's not feasible to label all the data. Oftentimes, fully labeling an entire training set is too costly and time consuming. Even if we can afford the time and money, there is simply too much data to label, to make the process a practical one.

➜ Reinforcement Learning

In reinforcement learning, the algorithm learns to perform a task by trying to increase the rewards it receives for its actions–doing more of the actions that get rewarded and doing fewer actions that do not get rewarded. So the question is, what does that mean in practice and how does it differ from supervised learning? Think of it this way: there is a defined outcome with supervised learning; we know what we want it to do, we know what we want it to find, and to a large degree, we tell it how to find it. With reinforcement learning, the method is more open ended, we allow the algorithm to explore many possible options and outcomes. When it comes up with something we deem to be good, we reward it. Rather than a passive learning exercise, it is an active one.

It's a three-step process: it takes an action, it receives a reward if the action is deemed good, and over time, the algorithm optimizes itself through self-correction. In short, the system is built to collect rewards.

We use the reinforcement approach in situations where the ideal end state cannot be clearly defined, potentially where only a small amount of training data is available and when you want to learn about the environment/situation by interacting with it.

We see reinforcement learning used regularly in robotics and industrial automation, with the load balancing of electricity grids and self-driving cars. We also see it used in the financial sector such as options trading. In all these situations, we know we want an optimal outcome, but exactly how to get that is unclear. We leave it up to the reinforced learning algorithm to explore the possibilities and find the best route.

→ Two Types of AI Applications

Just as there are different types of Machine Learning, there are different types of AI applications. Here we illustrate two of the more common applications of AI: Computer Vision and Natural Language Processing.

→ Computer Vision

Content is the lifeblood of business; traditionally, it has taken the form of documents, and more recently, web pages. But images and video are increasingly used both in social and business situations. Images can be anything from handwriting and signatures to faces or objects. AI plays a key role here in identifying and digitizing images. Handwriting recognition, through still a tricky area depending on whose handwriting is analyzed, is greatly enhanced by machine learning. Images, objects, and faces in images are now regularly detected and classified by AI.

This has repercussions beyond the use of these systems in social media: engineers are using AI to tag objects and structures in satellite images, doctors are doing the same in medical images, and lawyers are using AI to rapidly digitize handwritten statements and reports.

Automated image tagging and label generation has big implications for many use cases now and in the future. Until recently, images were poorly tagged (if at all) and were difficult to leverage as sources of content.

➜ Natural Language Processing

Just like images, speech has been a format of content that has been difficult to leverage in the past, but AI is rapidly changing that. For many (if not most) enterprises, speech files are hard to access and search. At best, they are tagged with a date and a basic title. As a result, many information managers have simply ignored speech as a form of content. But text-to-speech conversion, and more importantly (in information management terms), speech-to-text conversion has digitized and made speech a form of content that can be analyzed and managed.

This means that speech can be captured and rendered in chat bots. It enables us to understand different languages and generate translated content. The full implications of this in information management are still to be understood, but in an age of web conferencing and cell phones it could have a major impact on the scope of information management moving forward.

Moreover, AI goes further than simply digitizing speech; AI provides the tools to detect emotion or sentiment in speech, something that is of great interest to retailers, customer service, and law enforcement.

It also opens the door to more interactive digital assistants in the workplace.

→ Different Types of ML and AI

The lesson we really want you to take here is that not all forms of ML or AI are equal. Some types are better at doing certain things than others. However, the technology is getting better at everything at a rapid pace. For example, prior to 2009, AI struggled with speech and natural language understanding. For English it has made major strides; for many other languages, not so much. Historically, AI approached natural language in a rule-based manner: it figured out regular expressions, it used dictionary lookups and applied pure logic ("if this, then that" for example) to language. But of course, language is much more nuanced, organic, and flexible than that.

Similarly, it's only recently that AI has truly begun to really gain headway in computer vision—it's a fuzzy area (like language) that doesn't always reward a rule- and logic-driven approach to analysis.

In contrast, when it comes to Machine Learning, the technology you will be most likely to encounter will be pretty solid. It won't change a lot in the future. The difference between success and failure with Machine Learning is less due to the underlying ML technology, and more down to whether you supervised it properly and whether you provided it with good data. Machine Learning is reliant on your human intelligence, rather than true Artificial Intelligence.

So, the long and the short of this is that the technology continues to evolve. It is good at some things, better at others, but pretty darn good either way.

Key Points from this chapter:

1. AI can be applied almost anywhere from self-driving cars to drug discovery.

2. There are two main categories of AI use cases: exploratory and predictive.

3. Predictive AI predicts a business metric on what might happen next.

4. Exploratory AI use cases find patterns, categories, and groups.

5. Prescriptive AI is an extension of predictive AI, it advises on questions such as "What should we do next?"

6. AI is a catch-all term for a lot of different technologies, approaches, and tools.

7. Most AI systems are really Machine Learning systems. Machine Learning systems improve over time; they learn through experience.

8. True Artificial Intelligence systems are rare. They behave like humans and can sense, reason, act, and adapt to situations

9. Supervised learning uses training data and feedback from humans to learn.

10. In unsupervised learning, the algorithm in the system analyzes the data itself without human feedback and intervention.

2

Building an AI Strategy

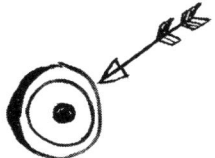

Now that you have an understanding of the types of Machine Learning and AI and what they can do, let's fast forward to leveraging that knowledge into developing a working strategy and roadmap for the use of AI for your organization.

Many organizations have an AI complex... it's a sexy topic, everyone is talking about it, so why aren't we doing it? We see many organizations where the most senior executives want or demand an AI strategy. That can be a good thing, as long as it's a strategy rooted in reality. But all too often the C-Suite may have grandiose plans and visions that need to be pared back. Nonetheless, if your most senior people are excited about AI you have their buy-in. Even if their ambitions need to be tempered, there should be forward progress.

At a business department level, you may have people asking for or exploring the use of AI. At the most superficial level, the marketing department may want to tell the world that you are leveraging AI. The product development team may be concerned that small startups might leapfrog them if they don't jump on the AI bandwagon quickly. And of course, the engineering or IT department may be simply wanting to play with machine learning to build out their personal skill sets.

Everyone is interested; each group is motivated differently, but the AI journey has begun. The first step in the journey needs to be taken with a solid understanding of what AI can and cannot do, ensuring everyone is on the same page. So, in this chapter we look at how your business can run and implement an AI system from start to finish.

Ensure you have this same reality check with your organizational team members. This is the starting point for any roadmap. Despite the hype, AI cannot do everything, and even some of the things it does, it does not do well. Conversely, when playing to its strengths AI can work near-miracles.

Fundamentally, AI identifies patterns; it searches data and arrives at decisions. It can be used to automate tasks and business processes. It can also augment existing processes and tasks, providing valuable insights and information.

What AI cannot do by itself is to be creative, to empathize. It cannot create a strategy for you and cannot improvise on the fly. Let's think about these limitations a bit further, taking empathy as our example. AI is being used extensively to automate call center work. It can do that well, but AI cannot empathize. It may be very efficient, but it's hardly likely to engage with or create any sense of relationship with the caller. It's a tradeoff: faster call-taking and question-answering, potentially weaker customer relationships.

You need to consider what AI/ML can really do well currently. For example, AI is good at narrow, focused tasks. AI performs poorly in broader situations, particularly those where there are many uniquely human capabilities. Consider this when creating a road map.

As a final point, consider why AI can automate even higher order knowledge workers like lawyers, traders, and radiologists, but struggles when it comes to roles like front office staff or salespeople. The fact is that the former, though highly educated workers, often perform the same functions and activities based on defined rules. In contrast, front office and sales workers require engagement, unscripted interactions, and relationship building. AI is good for narrow, focused tasks, particularly tasks that require high speed and sifting through large volumes of information. But the broader the task, the less focused and clear the outcome with AI will be. AI starts to falter with tasks that really require some kind of human intervention. The key point is that everyone in your team, and indeed anyone of relevance in your organization, needs to understand the limitations at the start of the project

➡ Are you really being left behind in the AI race?

Another area you and your team need to consider when building strategy is to consider where your organization is currently at in the adoption of AI. Here, we get another dose of reality thrown into the mix. All those people who say AI is already having an impact on their business and all those that think it will have a big impact soon? Well, the reality is that most haven't done anything related to AI yet. Our research indicates that roughly a quarter of the organizations that have initiated AI projects, are only in the pilot stage. So, if you thought you were being left behind, you are probably not. You are probably with the majority. And if your organization has already adopted AI, then good for you! You have a head start.

➡ Planning for Problems

Whether you are some ways down the track with AI or haven't started yet, you will encounter barriers along the way. Again, these barriers to adoption are important to acknowledge and plan for. The most obvious barrier to adoption is attracting and developing the right AI talent. It's in short supply, and worse, many people who claim to be AI experts are no such thing. You will need technical resources and you may not have these in-house; some may come from your AI supplier, others from third-party developers or system integrators. But that's not the whole story - the purpose of this book is to enable business people to feel confident about owning, running, and being responsible for AI in their organization. We call them "Practical AI Experts". Not just computer science PhDs, but such practical AI experts are also in tremendous short supply. The good news is that by picking up this book you have shown your intent to increase your practical chops in AI. Our guess is that there are few (if any) others in your organizations with a similar desire to understand the opportunities and challenges that AI brings, let alone how to deal with them when they inevitably arise.

Then there is the issue of security. In this context we are not just talking about the security of the AI system and its data—it's broader than that. Regulatory compliance, privacy, and legal issues come into play. These should not be show stoppers for any AI project, but if you fail to adequately plan for at least some involvement of security, legal, and privacy folk in your planning stages at a minimum, then they can be.

It certainly should not come as a surprise that there will likely be cultural resistance to AI within your organization. AI speaks to automation, and all automation projects since the dawn of time have engendered resistance. So, expect and plan for that.

You need to make AI a priority, and the early steps in this chapter should give you some tips as to how to do that and to raise awareness with decision makers why the time to act is now.

"OK, OK, I get it!" you are probably saying at this point! AI is everywhere, anything I do is part of something bigger. But what about my specific project? How do I get started with AI in my business? Don't worry, that's what we will talk about now. However, that context was important and feeds into what comes next.

The first question you need to consider is: what are the specific business drivers for your AI project?

In a broader context, the likelihood is that you are driven by a desire to gain or sustain a competitive advantage, or to enter into new areas of business, stave off competitors, etc. Those are important business drivers, but if everyone is getting into AI then they could arguably be table stakes. AI (as this book has already shown you) is a long-term investment and you need to think beyond the short term. Assume that your competitors and future competitors in adjacent markets are also at least considering the use of AI to keep parity. Reducing costs is a key driver—but just as important and just as overlooked is the fact that in the not-too-distant future both your suppliers and your customers will be expecting you to leverage AI. You need to think holistically about the short- and long-term drivers, both for the internal and external factors that affect your business.

A wide range of industries believe that AI is already starting to have an impact today, but there is an element of common sense at work here. More believe that the true impact will come over the next few years. Many in the early stages of exploring or deploying AI in their organizations are coming to realize that the impact of AI is cumulative and comes over time. Initially the impact may be small, but it compounds year after year. So, you need to ensure that you get started early enough. AI takes time and many others are already part way along the track.

Now, the impact of AI on business processes gives us some cause for concern. Everyone appears to agree AI will have a big impact on processes, but many seem to think this impact will come further down the line. In reality, even a small change in a process can have a big impact on a worker's or department's daily life. It depends on how you define a big impact. AI can have an immediate impact on the day-to-day work of individuals, but it may take time for the results of all those small changes to have a big impact on the business as a whole. You need to plan for an immediate impact on your processes, as well as the greater impact AI will have in the mid and long term. Your processes will change, and hiccups and push backs not identified or mitigated against at the start could derail your project

Finally, let's consider your existing business operations; for example, your sales, HR, procurement, accounts, marketing processes, etc. To you these may seem to be straightforward and discrete activities. An AI system may not view these things as so clear-cut; it may see more optimal ways of working, it may not respect the cultural silos that exist within your organization. Outside of very narrow, niche projects, the use of AI will likely have a knock-on impact, including potentially unexpected impacts, across your organization. Remember when we said that you need to think holistically when planning the use of AI? Well, consider the chain effect of automating decision-making in one aspect of your business and how that may affect other areas of your business.

You must ask three essential questions:

1. What is the project? What value will it bring? What impact will it have?

2. What will the project involve in terms of changes to existing systems, processes, and the organization?

3. What financial benefits will the project bring?

Depending on the answers to those questions, your leadership will meet and decide whether to go forward or not.

➡ Costs to Consider

Like IT projects, staff costs are a significant chunk of the overall costs. Because of a talent shortage in certain areas, the salaries for AI specialists can be higher than other IT roles. Also, seemingly basic tasks like labeling of the training data can be a significant cost.

In AI projects, you also will have to budget for data and computing environment costs. Plus, if your teams need any external consulting support for opportunity identification, roadmap development, and working alongside the team, that cost also has to be considered.

In contrast to normal Central Processing Units (CPU) in our computers and laptops, Graphical Processing Units (GPU) are special purpose hardware chips that are needed to optimize many machine learning applications. Another special purpose hardware chip is the Tensor Processing Unit (TPU), which is optimized for certain machine learning applications.

GPUs/TPUs can make your machine learning applications run faster, but keep in mind that they can be more expensive compared to normal CPU-based environments. Though these should not break the budget, if you need them you will have to budget for them.

The likelihood is that your AI project is going to be processing a lot of data, fast. You may decide to use optimized on premise servers or utilize cloud services such as Amazon, Microsoft or Google. Either way, you need to budget carefully. We suggest you do a five-year cost analysis as low monthly fees can stack up versus high initial costs for on premise hardware.

Finally, it's worth repeating that most AI projects will use some kind of external consulting and this can also be expensive. However, there can be great value in engaging experts that have AI project experience, saving you from reinventing the wheel.

This is the budget in the initial phases when you are about to begin your AI journey.

After that, you will need to factor in solution deployment, solution management, and solution retraining costs.

AI projects may require (indeed, we strongly recommend that they do) extra governance and specialist oversight teams. In fact, AI projects will almost certainly be staffed differently to traditional IT projects, and the vendor partnerships you will form will have deeper and different dimensions to them than is traditionally the case.

And of course, AI projects will require a significant amount of change versus the status quo. Change may well be profound and any change, no matter how small, needs to be managed.

AI is about radical change, automating the decision-making process within your organization. Therefore, any AI project is by default a tool to be used in broader business change activities. There are exceptions again, in the most niche of augmentation cases, but keep this in mind. AI is used for organizational change and its impact may well reach beyond one process or department.

→ Selecting AI Projects

So, if those are things to consider, how do you select an AI project in the first place? Here we provide some pointers for you to follow in the process.

Is the business task you are considering applying AI to data-driven, and if it is, do you have access to the necessary data? Consider that much of the data utilized in that task today maybe in employees' heads rather than in a database.

Ask yourself whether AI is overkill: do you really need the scale of automation that AI provides or are there simpler ways to improve the status quo?

Don't focus on the AI technology itself. Focus on the functionality it provides: does this align with the business needs? Understand that AI algorithms are there to support the business. AI is a means to an end, not an end in itself.

→ Which Use Cases?

Though every organization tends to consider itself to be unique, in reality there are common use cases. That's good, because you can learn from others and leverage best practices and technologies that have been optimized for these use cases.

Document automation, recommendation systems or the detection of fraud are all common use cases for which AI can be effectively utilized. In fact, these three are the most common use cases today, as they cover a lot of potential business situations and can deliver quick returns on your AI investment. We are seeing a big rise in the use of text and speech in the automation of customer interactions, particularly in call centers and field service—expect that to grow even further over the next few years.

Computer Vision refers to enabling computers through AI to understand the content of images or videos and opens the door to a whole new world of intelligent information management. Compared to the other use cases here, adoption of Computer Vision may be still in its early days, but such automation of visual recognition tasks is poised to be the next big thing. We will see its use grow in engineering, manufacturing, healthcare, and retail.

Similarly, we see several use cases in the world of online customer interactions, such as text and speech recognition and analysis. We use text analytics to read emails and call transcripts, surfacing any issues that may arise in those communications. Or we can translate speech into text for analysis or even analyzing customer and agent voice conversations to understand sentiment.

We are seeing a big uptick in the exploration of AI to detect emotion and better respond to customers in real time. Remember, though, that AI cannot really empathize, it can only fake (or simulate) empathy. Though this is important, it's a tricky area to explore.

Similarly, we are seeing more use of image and video analytics—that can be used to analyze brand images in social media to understand customer sentiment, or to analyze the movement of customers through the consideration, selection and buying process.

Many of these use cases in customer experience can also be applicable within the enterprise with employees, partners, or suppliers.

As you can see there are multiple use cases, but it's a finite list. We are not saying that the lists here are exhaustive, but they cover the majority of use cases we see both within the enterprise and the world of customer experience. They should be your starting point on your roadmap development journey.

→ AI Roadmap

So, with that let's dive into the world of the AI roadmap...

Now that we have a sound foundation of what AI can and cannot do, we get to four key components:

- → Define goals

- → Define use cases

- → Identify team needed

- → Identify the data required

Business goals: First, you need to define and understand how you will measure your business goals: what metrics, what KPIs (key performance indicators) are we trying to improve? Define these first, and be clear what goals your AI is focused on achieving or exceeding.

Use cases: Secondly, define the use cases: document the function, the process, the application, and the method you will employ.

Team: Third, sketch out the AI team: what roles and skills you require? What you already have and what you will have to draft in? Also consider governance: legal, compliance, and ongoing monitoring and supervision. Governance won't happen without defined and identified roles and skills in place.

Data: Finally, work out the data you will need: where it's going to come from and what platforms, products, and tools you will require.

Always approach the technology enablers after you have identified your goals, your use cases, and your team. Too many AI projects start with product selection and pay a heavy price as a result.

Those of you that have been involved in technology projects before may be a little confused at this point. "Where are the milestones and follow-on projects?" you may ask. As we stated at the outset, AI projects are very different to traditional IT projects where you sequence projects over a number of years. With AI it's all up-front work, then lots of monitoring and tweaking going forward. Many AI projects fail as people try to manage them the traditional way. As you will see throughout this book, AI has to be handled in its own specific way.

Taking our road map to the next stage, we will look at the major tasks that IT and the business roles will undertake. By definition, the IT folk are going to run the machine learning process. IT will take the use cases that the business has identified. They will then prepare the data, evaluate the model, pilot, tune, and iterate the model, and ultimately deploy to production.

The business needs to be involved closely in the vendor and technology selection, and of course staffing and continuously evaluating the strategy. The bottom line here is that it's easy to think that AI projects are IT or data science heavy. In reality, they are equally balanced between the business and IT–if one dominates the other, things will go wrong quickly.

Key Points from this chapter:

1. Start out small and focus your project on a short-term return on your investment. Be wary of overly ambitious projects. You must work in small, incremental steps.

2. Think of narrow applications and tasks where you can apply AI, and be sure that the business drives both the business plan and the use cases you select rather than IT.

3. Be sure to tightly define the problem you are trying to resolve and the scope of your AI project. Scope creep can sneak in very quickly in AI.

4. Always make sure that you inventory the available data and identify the data gaps before moving ahead too quickly. If you don't have the data, you can't move ahead.

5. Even if you have the data, make doubly sure you do a human sense check of that data to make sure it's of sufficient relevance and quality for you to use.

6. If it is relevant and good data, consider what can realistically be learned from analyzing it. Again, what gaps or limitations might there be with the data?

7. You also need to do a reality check (many do not) and simply consider if this task is really learnable.

8. Don't underestimate how much data may be in employees' heads and experience. Without that, you may be going down a dead-end road.

9. Assuming everything is looking good, consider how you will utilize the AI in your workflow. How will it integrate with real-world tasks and activities?

10. Finally, be sure to consider regulatory compliance impacts on your project.

3

How It Works, Step-by-Step

We have been talking a lot about AI. Now, it's time to get more specific. Machine Learning includes Deep Learning, which is the use of artificial neural networks that are loosely modeled after the human neural system (more about this later.)

If this is already starting to sound a bit confusing, don't worry. We have a full section to come that is devoted to the various branches of AI and machine learning. Here, we will keep it fairly simple. Machine Learning follows a fairly standard sequence of six steps that are outlined below.

→ Step 1: Problem Definition

The very first thing we need to do is define the problem we are trying to resolve. You really cannot underestimate the importance of this first step! Describe in detail the problem and identify any assumptions. This can be a great team exercise, similar to a brainstorming session. Consider how the proposed solution to the problem will be used and the benefits it will provide. Then, go further and describe how this same problem could be solved manually. This part of the step is perfect to help surface existing domain knowledge and identify data requirements.

→ Step 2: Data Preparation

AI is all about data preparation. You need to figure out what data is available, what is needed, and what isn't needed. You also need to figure out what might be missing. Once you have identified your data, you need to format, clean, and sample the data to make it ready for use. This may involve some data transformation, where you take data that has already been processed and aggregate it with other data, decomposing it or scaling it further—in short, getting it ready for the machine learning model.

→ Step 3: Apply Machine Learning

Now that you have your data, you need to apply machine learning algorithms to that transformed data. Be aware that there may not be one best algorithm for your needs. You may need to try out several different algorithms and pick out a few that look promising, with a view to further optimizing them at some point. One of the most common approaches here is to split the data into a training and a test subset. You train the algorithm on the training portion, then evaluate its performance on the test version.

→ Step 4: Tune the Model

If you expected everything to be perfect after step three, then you are likely in for a disappointment. Now, you need to tune the models. You will need to tune the data and algorithms, and possibly also combine multiple models to get to your optimized state.

➡ Step 5: Deploy the Model

At step five, you actually get down to deploying the machine learning model. It's also the point where the IT infrastructure team really gets involved in taking the model into the production environment. They will consider aspects such as scalability, load balancing, hardware requirements, security, and auditability.

➡ Step 6: Monitor the Model

Now that the model is in production, it needs to be monitored post-deployment for performance and to manage any new versions of the model if they are updated.

These six steps describe how Machine Learning works. It is important to grasp the flow of these steps, as this defines how you will work with Machine Learning in your own projects. These steps mean nothing without data to use and process, of course. So, it's the data we are looking at next.

Building a Data Strategy

AI value is not derived from technology (software) alone. To a large extent, it is based on data: good quality data, and lots of it. Yes, algorithms are important, and having access to the right software and hardware infrastructure to process data is also important. But without data (and typically a lot of it), nothing is going to work. No matter how smart the algorithm, no matter how great your on premise or cloud infrastructure, without good data you have nothing. With that out of the way, let's figure out an approach to a great data strategy.

The growth of AI has been in large part due to the huge volumes of easy-to-access data. Models tend to improve with more data, so the search is always on for more data or for the model to generate additional data. But *clean* data is just as important as *more* data. You need to ask if the data you have is the right data. Is it full of outliers? If so, can these outliers be eliminated? More volumes of data may not be the answer to everything; filling in missing critical small gaps in the data may be more important. Similarly, some data may not be needed at all. In fact, your model may be more efficient without it. So, as you move forward, rather than simply going down the "more is best" path, you may want to consider aggregating or even gradually getting rid of some existing data and features.

If you think you have great data already that you can simply dump into your machine learning environment, this might change your mind. Data scientists spend the majority of their time cleaning and organizing data—the work of building training sets and refining algorithms is a small part of their work. Data is messy. It needs to be managed, and you need a strategy for that. A good data management strategy frees up your most scarce and valuable resources.

To build a data strategy, we first need to categorize the challenges of data. Our approach is to categorize into four groups: availability, accessibility, usability, and data understanding. Let's look at each.

→ Data Availability

A good data strategy starts with a data inventory. Is the data actually available to you? If not internally available, can you acquire the data externally from another source? Usually, this is not a black and white situation. Some data is usually available, but it is typically missing some important pieces. Most likely because historically, we did not collect data with the intention of using it in machine learning. So even though there may be some data available, it may need to be augmented with new data to make it usable for machine learning. Here are some things to consider:

When it comes to data accessibility, even if the data is available, there can be difficulties actually getting your hands on it. Department heads or external customers may not have given permission for the data to be used. It's quite possible that the data contains personally identifiable information, and so regulatory or security rules prevent you from accessing that data. There can also be the simple challenge of delays in getting hold of valid data, as data teams tend to be busy and you may not be a priority for them.

How usable is the data if we can get a hold on it? Is there enough data? How much is enough for our purposes? How accurate is the data? How well structured and labeled is it? To go back to the volume question, volume requirements vary with the type of use case. Sometimes you have lots of data, but there is not enough variety in the data. Say you have a million rows of data. That's great, but if those million rows represent only 30% of possible outcomes or customer paths, then it is not enough data. Data may not be missing, but it may be messy, e.g. typos or different spellings of the same label. Data quality checks at collection stage can help, but otherwise you'll spend a lot of time cleaning up data.

Finally, let's look at data understanding. We are not talking here about business knowledge, but rather things like understanding what each column of data means (column names can be cryptic when you have hundreds of columns). A lot of guesswork is involved in understanding what a column name means in a spreadsheet or

Practical Artificial Intelligence | *An Enterprise Playbook*

data repository, particularly if you are not getting data from the direct source. Schema definitions can help a bit. Here, ongoing collaboration between machine learning and business analyst teams is important.

We see that to get a machine learning project started, a lot of ad-hoc data preparation happens. But machine learning projects need data on an ongoing basis—high-quality data needs to be fed to the model consistently. One-off or ad-hoc approaches don't scale. You need to think about not just the data you need to kick the project off, but what you will require in the future to continue to feed the model. This may all seem quite tactical, but we raise it here as all this work and the challenges involved need to be recognized and addressed in your planning and strategy work. All too often, they are not.

→ Data Best Practices

We just categorized and discussed the challenges of data and the things that need to be considered in building a data strategy. Here, let us look at how others have been managing or addressing those same problems and provide some best practices. Bear in mind that these challenges of accessibility, availability, usability, and understanding are not random. They are the result of a lot of real-world trial and error. What follows are practical ways that you can overcome these challenges

→ Create a data inventory. Understand and document what additional data you might have to acquire to augment your core data.

→ Create a data pipeline. Remember you will need to keep feeding data to the model over time.

- Ensure that the data you locate is actually available to you, that you can actually get your hands on it. Gain a solid understanding of the security controls around sensitive data. Be sure you have customer consent to use the data if it includes personally identifiable data, etc.

- Be sure to plan to assess the usability of the data. It won't be perfect; you will need to do something to get it into a form that you can use. So again, plan for that.

- Ensure that your machine learning experts, the data owners, and the business teams work together to ensure the data is understandable for machine learning work. Once again, plan for this.

Sounds simple? Actually, it can be if you plan and are aware of these steps in advance. Don't just grab data and assume it's going to be fine; there is a process to follow to ensure that it is.

→ Deployment and Management

First of all, we are going to think about deployment and model management best practices and challenges. Let's start with the challenges that surround deployment.

As we say in many places in this book, AI has only recently started to make inroads into the mainstream of business. As such, model deployment is a relatively new area for many data science teams. Until recently it was outside of their scope, so there is typically going to be a learning curve to go through, and things can go wrong. In addition, models have been developed in multiple different languages and frameworks and may be from different devices and environments, complicating further the model deployment. One of the outcomes of this complexity may be challenges in meeting security and audit requirements.

Thankfully, there are emerging best practices for complex model deployment. Most notably, it is now considered best practice to use common software development best practices such as continuous integration and continuous deployment for machine learning models. In practice this means the safe automation of the build and the testing of code every time that someone makes a change. It's also now considered a best practice to use micro-services and serverless capabilities to ensure scalability and modularity of the system. Add to this the best practice of monitoring system performance metrics like latency and error rates, and many of the risks of deployment can be mitigated.

When it comes to machine learning models themselves, a big challenge (particularly in large organizations) is that often, multiple teams are building different models from scratch. This results in different teams duplicating work and you'll end up with different versions of the same model!

Simple but effective best practices are critical here. You need to create a central registry for model discovery and re-use. You also need to ensure that you automatically version models as they are deployed and retrained.

Together, these best practices (if followed correctly) should save you from a lot of heartache.

→ Algorithms and Infrastructure

Now, let's look at best practices related to algorithms and infrastructure.

Let's start with the algorithms aka machine learning methods. The same general approach should be taken for algorithms: the most complex may not necessarily be the best. The best algorithm for you is the one that best captures the core requirements of your business problem. The good news is that you are probably not the first to tackle this for a similar business problem. It's a good idea to review (or get someone on your team to review) the academic literature to find out which algorithms achieved the best performance for the type of problems you're looking to solve.

Next, let's look at the topic of ensemble methods, which combine predictions from multiple models. There is a (silly) joke going around that asks, "If you ask three AI systems the same question, what do you get?" The answer is (and you have probably guessed this already) three different answers. It's worthwhile to compare, contrast, and combine outputs from multiple methods (referred to as ensemble methods) to arrive at a better prediction.

→ Human in the Loop

At this point we need to clarify that there are two areas of human supervision in AI. We use "human in the loop" processes to involve real people in resolving exceptions thrown out by the AI. It's a smart approach and can substantially improve the effectiveness of machine learning models.

Most enterprises do not have a lot of labeled data even though they may have a lot of data, as the labeling of data is quite time and resource intensive. AI requires labeled data sets to work, particularly in supervised machine learning situations.

Supervised machine learning refers to training models on labeled data sets. To be clear, supervised machine learning is used in the vast majority of the AI use cases currently being used in enterprises.

(For clarity, let's note that unsupervised learning operates on unlabeled data trying to identify hidden groupings and patterns.)

Human in the loop (HITL) is a semi-supervised machine learning method. HITL is deployed in use cases where there is lots of inexpensive unlabeled data, but the cost of labeling is expensive. The underlying philosophy here is that machines can learn more economically if they ask humans for some context. In a sense, human workers and machines complement each other's efforts in a single loop.

In principle it's a simple process; once a model has been deployed, it goes about its work. If the model is confident about its prediction, it proceeds as normal. In cases where it is not so confident, it will refer that instance to a human who will do the analysis for it. That human analysis is fed back into the training model so that next time the same exception occurs, the machine will know what to do with it.

In theory, the use of HITL decreases over time as the exceptions are identified and resolved. In some cases, though, as the system advances more exceptions may be identified. Things change in the real world over time, and the human remains in the loop for a much longer time.

Note that there is the much broader and important topic of overall
supervision of an AI system. AI systems can be incorrect.
The AI doesn't know it's incorrect – it has processed the data as you
requested it to. However, it may be reflecting biases we didn't initially
know were in the data. Moreover, it may just be that something is
wrong with the model. Humans are often good at intuitively knowing
when something doesn't look right and can step in to find out what is
wrong and take corrective actions.

Human supervision of AI is a best practice and we urge you all to take
that route. Ensure your AI is supervised by humans, as even the best
AI can sometimes start to go awry. If the problems are not picked
up early enough, they can be difficult to unravel. In some cases,
supervision may even be mandated by law.

Key Points from this chapter:

1. Machine Learning systems follow a series of six steps: problem definition, data preparation, applying machine learning, tuning the model, deploying the model, and monitoring the model.

2. You need a data strategy with access to lots of high-quality data.

3. Data scientists spend the majority of their time cleaning and organizing data.

4. The data you need may not be easily accessible or usable.

5. Machine learning systems need to be fed data on an ongoing basis.

6. Create a data inventory and pipeline.

7. Ensure your experts, data owners, and business teams work together to ensure the data is usable and understandable for machine learning work.

8. Use best practices such as continuous integration and continuous deployment.

9. The biggest and most complex algorithm may not be the best for your needs.

10. AI systems tend to require 'humans in the loop' to resolve exceptions. You should plan for that.

4

Methods of Machine Learning

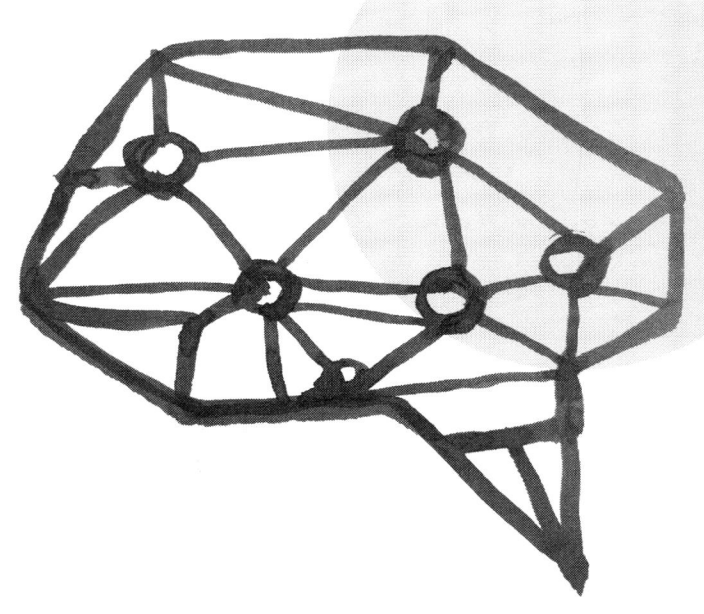

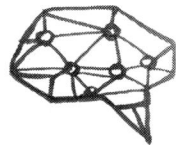

O
ur next step down the path is to understand the different methods we can use in Machine Learning, as there are many different methods to choose from when implementing AI. This is not something that is obvious if you are to read or listen to technology vendor marketing. Sometimes it feels as if technology vendors think buyers are too dense to understand the differences between different ML tools and approaches.

Few buyers ever ask how the ML actually works or what methods it uses, but as you will see in this section of the book, the differences between ML methods are quite easily understandable. Some methods follow a simple question-and-answer approach, others use statistical analysis, and yet others mimic the way the human brain works. You don't need to understand the underlying mathematics behind these differences, but a basic understanding of the differences and where one fits where another may not is invaluable. To be honest, this stuff can get complicated quickly, so we have tried our best to explain each of the major methods in layman's language. No prior experience or mathematical expertise needed!

Let's step through each method one at a time and explain what each can do and how they differ. This is the most technical section in the book but bear with us, our goal here is simply to illustrate the different approaches and methods. Even a limited level of understanding of the differences can be of great value when selecting the right methods and technologies for your own project. Remember that even if you don't read this all at once, it is here for you as a reference tool at any future point in discussions with technology vendors or your own data scientists. We will start with a concept called linear regression, then move on to some of the more common ML methods used today.

→ Linear Regression

Rough Translation:
If this happens, then that will happen

Linear Regression is one of the most fundamental and simple methods used in machine learning, and requires supervised learning. Linear Regression is commonly used for forecasting and for identifying the cause-and-effect relationships between two or more variables. We can go as far as to say it is a fundamental building block for predictive analysis. In mathematical terms, it is the relationship between X and Y.

For example, we might count the number of employees in a company (input variable X) to the firm's revenue (output variable Y). Assuming there is a strong correlation between these two, we can predict future revenue based on the number of employees. In reality we might add more variables to increase the accuracy of our prediction, but you get the idea. Another example is email spam filtering. We might relate the content of the incoming email with variables related to other known spam messages. With linear regression methods, we are trying to understand the relationship of one (or more) input variables to another output variable.

The key to success with linear regression is ensuring there is a strong correlation between X and Y, otherwise things will go awry quickly. Statisticians have a nice way of explaining this concept: they call the X variable the *explanatory* variable, and the Y variable is called the *response* variable. One explains the parameter that changes – i.e. the content of the spam email–while the other provides the response – i.e. "Is this a spam message?"

Linear regression is a solid fundamental method for predicting outcomes, but it needs careful supervision. It's of little use in doing anything other than forecasting outcomes.

→ Logistic Regression

Rough Translation:
Black or White?

Logistic regression is based on the same basic principles of linear regression, but with logistic regression the possible outcomes are limited. In linear regression the outcomes can have a number of variables; in other words, there is an infinite number of possible outcomes. With logistic regression, the outcomes are binary. For example, is it black or is it white? Is a customer likely to repay the loan or not? Is a skin lesion malignant or benign? So again, Logistic Regression is similar to linear regression, but with only two possible outcomes. This is a powerful method used regularly in machine learning, but hopefully you can see that it has limitations. It is great in binary situations, but of no use in situations where there are multiple possible outcomes.

→ Linear Discriminant Analysis

Rough Translation:
We know this, so now we know that

We use the Linear Discriminant Analysis method when we know and have defined a number of groups or clusters that we want to classify beforehand, and then want to classify new data points based on some defined criteria. An example of this would be when we want to segment customers into regular, high-spending individuals versus irregular, lower-spending customers.

To put it another way, we use this method to find a combination of features that characterizes (or separates) two or more classes of outcomes. In our example above, we might consider features such as salary, location, past spending patterns, membership of loyalty schemes, credit card usage etc. to separate those that are likely to be high spenders in the future versus those that will not. We would use a number of features in our analysis, as wealthy people are not necessarily high spenders, whilst lower-income people may ironically be high-spending target customers for our product or service.

→ Decision Trees

Rough Translation:
If I do this, then that
And then this, next I will do that

Decision trees are a very popular regression type machine learning method. It's one of the easier methods to grasp, as it essentially just answers a hierarchy of yes or no questions until it arrives at an answer or decision.

Think of how you'd play a game like "Twenty Questions." Ultimately, it's a series of yes or no questions to get to the right answer. More practically, we might ask: Is an income higher than x? Are the outgoings lower than y? Did the income drop in the past year? etc. This is a simple but powerful and highly intuitive method that finds regular use in rules-based business activities like credit risk assessments, or for that matter, dating applications. It's pretty simple, and something we all do every day when we make decisions.

→ Random Forests

Rough Translation: This and That, plus This And That, plus That and This, Equals That

Random forests are a variation on decision trees. As the name might suggest, random forests are made up of lots of trees; they use multiple iterations of decision trees. Each individual decision tree in a random forest has its own data and its own path of yes or no answers to follow. Cumulatively, these individual decision trees can come together to improve the accuracy of a traditional single decision tree.

For example, analyzing customer churn for your products and services will involve many interrelated factors based on your actual knowledge of the customer and their patterns of behaviors related to other customers etc. Factors in the decision tree analysis of customer churn might include things like the type of contract the customer has, their payment history patterns, whether they have used the customer support service, how much they have used your service, how they have used your service etc.

Hence, using multiple decision trees in a random forest makes sense in situations like these and hopefully provides more accurate predictions and analysis. It is also worth noting that one of the big advantages of using decision trees and random forests is the ease of interpreting them. It's pretty straightforward to understand why it comes to its decisions, as it followed a series of yes or no questions to come to a conclusion.

→ Naïve Bayes

Rough Translation:
This is probably the right answer

Bayes was a 17th Century English statistician who discovered some important statistical theorems, including a method we call Naïve Bayes. But that's just a bit of history—you want to know what it can do and how it works.

Naïve Bayes uses something called probability theory. It calculates probabilities or likelihoods of events occurring based on not just fixed past events, but also on new information that we receive over time.

Imagine you are trying to automatically classify a document or a news article. Naïve Bayes looks at all the possible classifications available and predicts the most likely classification. It does that by considering all the past information and features it has of similar documents or news articles. It considers all this, and decides with some certainty that this is probably an invoice or an article about rugby league.

➔ Support Vector Machines

Rough Translation: This is probably the right anwer – Or it could be THAT

Support Vector Machines (SVM) are a highly popular supervised classification technique. The name is a bit obtuse, but it is another linear classifier that classifies data into different groups. It is this or it is that–it's news about Syria or it's news about Iran, for example. In fact, this approach is a little smarter than just A versus B classifications (Is this an invoice or a news article about rugby league?), as it also recognizes a buffer region around the classification lines. In other words, it can say that this may possibly be this, or it may possibly be that. SVMs can define with certainty but they can also make what we might describe as an informed guess even when it is not 100% certain. Most often, SVMs analyze large amounts of data to detect patterns within them. The patterns may not be identical, but they are similar enough to decide that this is probably a nose, a cat, or the letter W. Accordingly, you might use SVMs to detect a face, classify an image, or to recognize handwriting.

➔ Ada Boost

Rough Translation: I have weighed all the different opinions and decided that...

"Ada Boost" is short for Adaptive Boosting; it's a technique that uses multiple models to come up with multiple decisions, and then weighs them against one another based on the accuracy of their predictions. Think of it this way: all of the models may have their strengths and weaknesses depending on the situation, but Ada Boost sequentially considers each model's suggestions and weighs those suggestions to deliver a high-quality outcome. To put it another way, Ada Boost considers the merits of a number of somewhat questionable ML outputs to come to an overall balanced decision. A typical use case for AdaBoost is also in image classification, where there are many different images, shapes, colors, tones, and structures to consider.

→ Gradient Boosting Trees

Rough Translation: I took a guess, but now with more information I have changed my answer

Gradient Boosting shares some similarities to Ada Boost because it also uses a combination of different analysis structures. In gradient boosting, though, it's not different models but different decision trees. Think of this as a sequence of decision trees somewhat like Random Forests, but in Gradient Boosting each decision tree tries to correct the errors from the previous tree and improve the outcome. The final output combines the results from all the previous trees. It's a technique that can be used in inventory forecasting scenarios.

→ K-Means

Rough Translation: It looks quite a bit like an invoice, and less like a purchase order

K-Means is a system that divides a given dataset into a number of different clusters (K) by minimizing the distance between each data point and the center of the cluster to which the data point belongs to. To make sense of this, think of it this way: you have data that has features but no actual labels (it's sort of like this or sort of like that). What we can do, then, is find similar clusters of data that share some commonalities – they are not necessarily the same, but they are at least similar to one another.

When we find a number of these clusters, we can compare incoming data to figure out which cluster it is most like. This works well for content classification, for example: purchase orders (PO) may look different, but they share enough commonalities for the system to recognize that this is a PO and another piece of data is an invoice.

→ Hidden Markov Models

Rough Translation:
I can show you the way from my hiding place

Hidden Markov Models (HMM) are a machine learning clustering method that uses what are called hidden state analysis to predict observable states. This might sound confusing, but the concept is pretty simple: something hidden can point us to something we can see. Let's look at an example.

An example of a hidden state is high/low air pressure in weather predictions. By contrast, an example of an observable state is sunny/rainy weather. Another example of a hidden state could be the emotion *anger*; an observable state may be a lowered brow or a raised voice. Audio waves are also hidden states we can cluster and then associate with an observable state like specific sounds or words. The key thing here to understand is that one state is not visible but the output of that state is visible.

→ Summary

There are many different models and approaches used in ML and AI, but we have covered the most common approaches here. Each approach has a different application; an approach that is good for one thing will not do a good job in another situation. Some are more sophisticated than others, but the more sophisticated and complex the approach the more difficult it is to understand and unravel if something goes wrong. None of the above approaches are better than the others–it is about finding the right fit for your needs. If you need to know when to switch something off in an emergency, you might want to use a relatively simple linear regression method. On the other hand, if you want to detect objects in images then that won't work. The right tool for the right job is what's needed; a lawn mower is of little use to dig the garden, just as a spade is of little use to mow the lawn. Choose wisely, and ask some basic questions of any potential AI vendor or supplier about what models and approaches they use to ensure that it is a logical fit for your needs.

→ Neural Networks

Finally, we are going to dive into the world of Neural Networks, or more accurately, Artificial Neural Networks (ANNs). These are algorithms that are sort of modeled after the human brain/neurons– and perhaps is the right way to look at ANNs. Don't be fooled: they don't really mimic the way the human brain works. Let's debunk that myth before we go any further forward, as this misconception is at the root of many concerns regarding artificial intelligence. AI systems are reliant on ANNs, but they only mimic in a very basic way the processes of the much more complex human brain. Consider that a child's brain has 10 times the number of connections than the entire internet put together. Don't get us wrong; ANNs are very powerful, but they have a long way to go, if ever, to reach some kind of parity.

That being said, just like us, ANNs learn through examples. ANNs are analogous to how a child learns to recognize what a dog is from seeing examples of dogs, or to connect the sound of thunder with an incoming storm.

ANNs are simply a large interconnected and interactive network of learning tools (nodes). These nodes work together to take data inputs, process them in multiple steps, and provide outputs. ANNs undertake highly complex, advanced processing of data. They are often used in situations where we don't really know the exact input variables that influence the output or even the possible output. So, we hand that analysis and decision making over to this network of interactive nodes to figure it out for us.

With that, let's explore neural networks further in a technique commonly referred to as Deep Learning.

→ Deep Learning

The performance of machine learning algorithms depends heavily on the representation of data. Each piece of information in the data is known as a feature (somewhat similar to a column in a structured data table) and the machine learning algorithm learns how to use the features to extract patterns.

But often we don't know what features to extract. For example, we want to detect cars from an image. We may want to use the presence of wheel as a feature. But can you describe what a wheel looks like in terms of pixel values?

Wouldn't it be better if the algorithm learns features by itself with minimal human intervention? Deep learning does exactly that. It learns using a series of layers (networks of nodes), starting with pixels, to corners, to shape, to objects. Deep learning also does some heavy lifting in terms of extracting features from the data.

Practical Artificial Intelligence | *An Enterprise Playbook*

The concept of deep learning has been around for a long time, but it's only with the relatively recent access to vast amounts of data that are needed to build these deep architectures that deep learning has become a reality.

The depth and complexity of deep learning has huge promise and has already been shown to improve performance over many other machine learning approaches in a number of different application areas.

So, lots of data, lots of computing power, and many algorithmic layers in a neural network results in a very powerful learning system.

➡ Using Deep Learning

Image Recognition

Deep learning has led to breakthroughs in image recognition since around 2011. Prior to this, the state-of-the-art object recognition accuracy was in the low 70s percent range; it had an error rate of 26%. To contrast that with human judgement, we make errors around 5% of the time. So, the gap was huge.

By 2016, with the use of deep learning, that gap more than closed– it had surpassed human recognition. State-of-the-art image recognition systems now have an error rate of only 3% for the things they are trained on. That's an important caveat–humans can recognize many more things than a machine, but for those that both the machine and the human have been trained to recognize, the machine can now do the job better than the human. Amazing? Scary? A bit of both...

Deep learning can comfortably outperform traditional machine learning methods. For example, with deep learning we can gain a 41% reduction in errors for image classification over traditional machine learning and a 27% error reduction on facial recognition etc. You might be asking why don't we use deep learning for everything if it's so amazing. There are lots of reasons really, but remember the vast volumes of data it requires? That's hard to get hold of.

➜ Deep Learning Applications

Despite these challenges, the power of deep learning has opened up several new applications. For example, it is now used for quality control, equipment maintenance, and monitoring across industries. These are limited and tightly defined environments that deep learning can observe and analyze in incredible depth. As it's a limited and closely defined environment, it also has a limited number of outcomes that it can respond to intelligently. When it comes to monitoring equipment for breakages or decay, this kind of situation is a perfect play for deep learning.

We have talked a fair bit about deep learning, which uses neural networks, but it's worth pausing here and breaking things down a little further to understand more thoroughly what a neural network is and how it is constructed. In the simplest of terms, a neural network architecture has three types of layers.

➜ *Input Layers* are the starting point. These are the nodes that bring data into the system for further processing.

➜ *Hidden Layers* are the layers that work on understanding and intelligently processing the data.

→ *Output Layers* are the layers that take the output of the hidden layers and parse them out into something useful.

As you can imagine, it's far more complex than this. Still, these three layers form the basic foundation for all neural network architectures.

For illustration purposes, let us consider that the input is an image (it could be any other data type, but we'll use an image, say that of a turtle, for this example). The image is then broken down into pixels.

Data from a pixel in the first (*input*) layer causes a node in that layer to signal its analysis to the nodes on the second layer and so on.

Every node in each layer will deal with a particular aspect of the picture, like edges, shadows, and shapes (*hidden layers*). The features are combined level by level until the final (*output*) layer categorizes the entire layer.

With a deep learning workflow, we start with a large set of features and output a small set of features. In the example we used above, we have an image that is made up of pixels. The hidden layers interpret particular patterns associated with other images of turtles, and in turn outputs millions of pixels down to the words "it's a turtle."

Similarly, data from an electronic sensor in a self-driving car might take many different pieces of data, conclude that what it is encountering is a pedestrian, and output a trigger to stop the car or swerve to avoid the pedestrian. An example that's closer to home could be an Amazon Echo or a similar device: when an audio stream is received by the device, the system detects amongst all that noise that you said the word "Alexa!"

➙ Types of Neural Networks

Until now, we have looked at neural networks as a standard structure: one of multiple input, hidden, and output layers. However, there are many different variations on neural network architectures, each geared to a specific use case. Each has its own pros and cons, and is optimized for different use cases. Let us look at some of these in more detail.

RNN

We are going to look at Recurrent (or Recursive) Neural Networks (RNN). The clue to understanding this one is in the name: *recurrent*. In a neural network, a node converts many inputs into a single output. But RNNs allow previous outputs to affect subsequent future inputs. In other words, they have a form of memory; they remember what happened previously and apply that to future processing work. Hopefully you can see why such an approach would be useful in things such as image classification.

RNNs are powerful, but like everything else they can have drawbacks. RNNs can be hard to train, and they may in fact learn many things you never expected them to learn. These things may not even be relevant to you and your work. The bottom line is that RNNs can become unruly. RNNs are black boxes; they are so complex in their computations that we may never really know how they learned or how they came to a decision.

LTSM

There are many other types of neural networks, such as Long Short Term Memory (LTSM). This is a type of neural network with greater memory control that allows for memory to persist or to be reset, avoiding the decay of any values passed from step-to-step. LTSM is often used for natural language processing.

CNN

Another is Convolutional Neural Networks (CNN), which preserves the spatial relationship between pixels by learning image features using small squares of input data. It's a system used for image recognition.

And many more...

Add to this a whole bevy of further acronyms like MLP, FNN, RBF, and MNN, and you get the general idea. The principle of layered networks of nodes, each involving three stages (input, hidden and output) is pretty standard, but just like the Machine Learning models we looked at there are many different options available each meeting a different need.

→ The Black Box Problem

All of these neural network architectures and methods are impressive, each in their own way, and can deliver amazing results. However, their sheer complexity and autonomy mean that we often end up with a *black box* neural network. What we mean by the term black box is that even though we know what data was input – for example, employment history, payment history, and demographics– we don't know how the neural network made the decision to decline or approve the loan application.

This raises the possibility of serious problems in terms of transparency, bias, and accountability. No matter how sophisticated the neural network or how much data it uses, there will always be a logic for the decisions they make–but we don't know what that logic is. That can be a big problem. We are going to look at this problem in more detail later in the book, but it is important to know that potential challenges exist in using neural networks. Deep learning can deliver dramatic improvements in performance over traditional machine learning, and it will improve further over time. Nevertheless, deep learning is very complex and can be very expensive, as it requires massive data sets, expensive consultants, and costly computing resources (GPUs). To add to all that, you have the issue that when it makes decisions you don't know why or how it came to that decision; that brings real and tangible business risks.

→ Keep Calm and Carry On

If this is all a bit difficult to grasp, just keep calm and carry on. Unless you are personally going to be building a machine learning or AI tool, it's not important that you fully grasp the differences between these different approaches. What is important is that you are aware that there are many different approaches, methods, architectures, learning tools, and neural networks. We are just touching on some of the different approaches to give you a flavor of what's out there. You may want to revisit and research more deeply the methods we have described. But in summary, one size definitely does not fit all. The method you end up using depends on the problem you are trying to solve. Next time somebody tries to sell you an AI system, you can be ready to ask some searching questions. It might not make you popular with the technology vendor, but it could save you from a lot of grief.

Key Points from this chapter:

1. There are many different Machine Learning methods you can use.

2. Linear regression systems are used to tell us *"If this happens, then that will happen."*

3. Logistic regression systems are used to tell us *"If something is this or that, black or white."*

4. Linear discriminant analysis systems are used to tell us *"If we know this, now we know that."*

5. Decision trees are used to tell us *"If I do this, then that, then this, then I will do that."*

6. Random forests are used to determine *"This and that, plus this and that, plus that and this, equals that."*

7. Naïve Bayes models are used to tell us *"This is probably the right answer."*

8. Support vector machines help us to understand *"This is probably the right answer, but it could be that."*

9. Neural Networks are loosely modelled after the human brain/neuron structure.

10. Deep Learning systems learn through a series of layers arranged as a network of nodes.

5

Running an AI Project

In this chapter we are going to cover all the basics of how to plan, staff, and execute an AI project. We are going to do something a bit different to the norm to kick things off, because AI projects, as you will see, are also a bit different. We are going to start by looking at some of the most common risks that are associated with AI and how you might mitigate those risks from the beginning. You need to be aware of the risks of using AI before you even get started with your project, so that you can go in with your eyes open.

→ Finding AI Skills

It is true that AI skills are in short supply, and that good AI skills are very hard to come by. But a common mistake we see firms make is that they think the real problem is in finding a good data scientist. And all too often, the AI-related education available today focuses on bringing us this new generation of data scientists. Your focus should not just be on data scientists; in fact, finding those might be the least of your problems. An AI project needs far more skills than those of a specialist data scientist. For example, an AI project needs DevOps experience–people who understand the real world of both IT and business, people who know how to develop and efficiently deploy AI in the real world.

You need people who can really dig deep to understand the underlying business challenges that you want to resolve, to understand and manage the business change that AI will involve, to deal with all the legal, privacy, and regulatory issues that might arise, and to manage what will be a differently structured and staffed project to traditional IT projects.

You may have to hire to fill these gaps. You may also want to consider training existing team members who already understand your operating environment and will remain with you far longer than an external consultant. You need to create a blended team that leverages traditional IT, business, and core AI skills. With that in mind, let's look at how AI projects differ from the normal IT projects you may be familiar with.

➜ How AI Projects Differ from the Norm

Think about the standard application lifecycle. The key stages of a traditional IT business application project go from design, to implement, to deploy and finally, support. This is a model and structure you may be familiar with, but this structure will not work for an AI project. That will come as a big surprise to many, and in turn it surprises us that this is not something discussed regularly and openly by AI vendors and practitioners. In an AI project, we have to fundamentally rethink the way things work.

So, what are the differences? What do we need to rethink? In a traditional software project, we make most of our important and difficult change decisions at the start of the project, when we design the software. We build and test the software, then we deploy it. Over time, we automate more of the work and address lower priority features in later releases. That is not at all how an AI project works.

The lifecycle for AI is starkly different. Firstly, it is not linear; rather, it is circular. There is no clear end point to your project. It never really ends. We create models, we train those models, test them, deploy them, monitor them, optimize them, then test and optimize over and over again. We experiment and continually go through this cycle of development and improvement with AI. On the surface, this may seem more onerous than the traditional application lifecycle. The twist is that it's not: you can get your AI application deployed more quickly, and you will continually improve the AI system over time.

Traditional applications are deployed and often do a great job in the short term, but then stuff happens, circumstances change, workarounds come into the equation, and the application's shortcomings are revealed. Over time, the use and value of the traditional application degrades, and eventually we end up looking for a replacement. We look for a new application that will work better than the last, one that can hopefully incorporate the lessons learned from the first time round.

On the other hand, with the AI lifecycle, we actually get an application that improves, rather than degrades, over time. In the short term there may be hiccups, but we have a continuous process of improvement in place that expects hiccups, one that is geared to fix them. We have an application designed from the get-go to improve and adapt on an ongoing basis. AI is in some regards the technical embodiment of continuous improvement. Each error is caught and is then used to improve the system. This way, the AI system itself learns over time, and with your help, becomes a better and better investment. It does not depreciate over time, it grows in value (in most cases, and if done right).

Practical Artificial Intelligence | *An Enterprise Playbook*

Let's explore that important concept in more detail. At the modeling stage for AI you will take a first shot at engineering the core features you require, and select and optimize your first model. Note that this is a first shot at the end solution; you know and expect that it will change over time. So, when you initially deploy your AI, you will closely monitor it when it goes to production and expect it to differ from your test environment.

With the knowledge you gain from that early performance, you will be able to run new experiments, features, and models. You will continue to go through this cycle over time. Each time you do, you will automate and improve further the retraining, the performance metrics, and the data. Though this cycle continues, it becomes a lighter and lighter burden as the AI learns, improves, and automates over time. This has major implications as to how you staff an AI project.

Such a different approach to the application lifecycle impacts the way you staff your project and system. For example, in traditional IT situations you will staff most heavily at the initial requirements and design stage. Once the application is implemented, you will dramatically drop the level of staffing, in some cases down to just one or two people or none at all, other than maybe a nominated support person. Let's look at how that differs in an AI situation.

In AI, it's the reverse of a traditional application lifecycle. With AI, you will typically staff more heavily from the deployment onward. In other words, you will staff up, not down. This is not an absolute—there will be peaks and troughs—but the principle holds true. You will require a small team to pull your requirements together. Things will really kick off at deployment. This is where things can go wrong if you don't staff sufficiently to monitor and optimize the system. You will want to keep that level of staffing for some time to come, and only drop the level of staffing as more elements are automated and the AI improves. But remember, AI will always need to be monitored, and you need to plan and staff for that.

→ Staffing Your Project

The first key risk we identified in the previous section was finding the right staff for your project, as AI skills are in high demand and qualified staff are hard to find. The problem is deeper than that; many projects get into trouble due to incorrectly staffing their projects. In our work, we have found that many organizations are surprised by the differences between traditional IT and AI project staffing requirements, and make fundamental staffing errors when designing and recruiting for their project. Let's dive in and see why.

We have identified the key roles you will need to fill for a typical AI project. Some you may have in-house, others you may need to hire for. You may want to engage a third-party consulting firm. It can be tempting to combine roles, but as we go through them you will see they are all require distinct skill sets.

Data Scientist

The data scientist is a critical role in any AI project, as a data scientist essentially does the work to translate a business problem into a machine learning problem. This is the role that will create the machine learning model and test it. This will also be the role that takes on the work of tuning the performance and optimization of the model over time. Data scientists (good ones, at least) can be hard to find. Once you have one you will likely want to keep them, as they will have an intimate knowledge of the machine learning model. You may want to hire or train somebody internally rather than engaging with a third party contractor.

Business Analyst

Most AI and IT projects succeed or fail due to the quality of the business analysis that is undertaken, yet we see this role being undervalued in organizations. In our opinion, good business analysts are worth their weight in gold. It is the business analyst that not only gathers the business requirements but also analyzes and defines the specific business problems. A good business analyst will have domain expertise, meaning that they intimately know your specific business. They also have subject matter expertise, meaning that they understand not only your business, but the in-depth processes and tasks involved in running the business. On the technical side of things, they will have a good grasp of the enterprise integration points and where internal data sources are located. A good business analyst provides a bridge between the real world of business and the technical domain of translating this into actionable requirements and definitions.

Data Analyst or Data Engineer

The data analyst is a role that undertakes the work of importing, exporting, and syncing all the data you require for your AI project. They are responsible for data cleansing and normalization; everyone's data is full of redundancy, junk, and duplications. The data analyst is also responsible for undertaking regular data quality checks. As we have stressed many times in this book, AI is all about good data, so it should be clear that a good data analyst is a critical addition to your team.

Project Manager

Every project needs a Project Manager, and AI projects are no exception. Make sure you have a skillful, qualified, and experienced project manager, as they will be the one responsible for ensuring that the project is delivered on schedule and on budget. To do that, they will require good management and budgeting skills. They will also be the one to manage all the various project dependencies and manage the risks. A good project manager is a taskmaster, but at the same time needs to be an excellent communicator and team player.

Machine Learning Developer

The next role you need to consider carefully is that of the Machine Learning Engineer or Developer. This is the person who will write all the machine learning code. They will also be the one to access and use open source machine learning libraries. This will be the person that uses cloud machine learning APIs. It's a specialist skill set, and you need to recruit with care.

Even More Roles

That's a lot of roles already, but as you can see there will be more to come, some of which you may be able to fill internally. For example, you may already have a UX (User Experience) designer in-house—UX is critical for AI, as any AI system is of little-to-no value if the people tasked with using it, struggle to use it. So, budget for both user experience and user interface skills.

Another role that needs to be filled is in the realm of IT operations and infrastructure. You will need a team to set the infrastructure and operating environment up to safely and securely deploy your machine learning applications.

Let's not forget that most AI projects will need privacy, legal, and compliance guidance, along with strong change management.

→ AI Team and Org Structure

Your AI team can be divided into the data group, the business group, and the machine learning group.

Your business group will be in charge of defining the use case, and in conjunction with the data team, exploring the features you require.

Your data group and machine learning group will create and publish features, build the model, and in conjunction with the business group, validate the models.

Each group has distinct roles to play, with the project manager ensuring that they collaborate effectively to ensure that the project is driven solely by the identified business goals.

Once a model has been deployed into production, these sub-teams (or at least individuals representing them) will stay involved, as the models will evolve over time. The models will need to be refined, the data augmented or changed, and business experts will be involved to ensure the business continues to benefit from the AI work.

Some AI teams will be large, others small, but all the roles we described need to be addressed. What also needs to be addressed is who this team reports to. This is where things can get difficult. It may seem logical that the team should report to the CIO, but as we have stressed multiple times, AI projects are really business projects that leverage AI technology. There is an equally valid argument that the AI team should report to the business unit to which the AI team is tasked with bringing improvements to.

There are no clear-cut answers to this one—each organization will view this situation differently—but whichever route you take, be sure to make the project as collaborative and broad as you are able to.

In larger organizations where there is an enterprise-wide strategy to utilize AI, each business unit should have its own dedicated team, with the CIO having a dedicated Center of Excellence team to guide, ensure consistency, and capture and leverage lessons learned.

What we caution against is in giving too many of these roles (or indeed the ownership of any teams) to outside consulting firms. These teams need to be collaborative and as close to the business processes and staff involved in those processes as possible. The team members also need to have longevity, as AI is an ongoing learning process. Outsourcing everything—or even significant chunks of work—to an outside firm can increase your risk exposure, and potentially leave big holes in both your knowledge and your ability to manage a project when the third party disengages or replaces its staff.

→ Defining Team Roles

You need specialist technical skills for data and machine learning, but you also need deep business expertise of your particular business. Like any project, there will be peaks and troughs of involvement: times when you need a core team, other times when you can scale back. This means that teams are going to be transient, and the skills required will change at times. Give a lot of thought to where you will get these skills from. Understand that you will need flexible access to them. Some skills you may have to bring in from outside your firm, but you should consider training in-house staff for many of the roles. In a sense, AI projects never really end, so consistency, knowledge of what has gone before, and a deep understanding of the data and business is essential and needs to be ongoing.

→ Project Management Methodologies

At this stage we have a grasp of the different roles for an AI project, the various skills of the team, and how the team may be structured. But what about a standardized methodology for project implementation? In other fields of IT, we have fairly well-defined methodologies. For instance, you may be familiar with ITIL for IT Infrastructure Management Projects.

Unfortunately, there isn't a single dominant methodology for AI projects. In fact, there isn't a single well-established methodology at all. This is perhaps because the way we are approaching AI projects is relatively new. Fortunately though, data mining and data science projects are closely related to AI projects, and there are some standard methodologies for data mining applications. Although they are used today for AI projects, we don't really recommend them.

Even so, let's look briefly at three of them here: KDD, SEMMA, and CRISDP-DM

Knowledge Discovery in Databases (KDD)

KDD refers to the broad process of finding knowledge in data and applying data mining methods. KDD is a five-stage process of Data Selection, Data Pre-Processing, Data Transformation, Data Mining, and Interpretation/Evaluation.

Sample, Explore, Modify, Model, Assess (SEMMA)

SEMMA was developed by SAS Institute, the long-standing vendor of analytics software. In theory it's independent of the Data Mining software chosen, but in practice tends to be most used when SAS software is being implemented.

Cross Industry Standard Process for Data Mining (CRISP-DM)

CRISP-DM was jointly developed by Daimler Chrysler, SPSS, and NCR in 1996. This is a well-adopted methodology and consists of six stages: business understanding, data understanding, data preparation, modeling, evaluation, and deployment. Though popular, there are a couple of disadvantages with CRISP-DM. Firstly, it was developed before the current-era big data and AI tools. Furthermore, the methodology has not been updated in recent years.

So, if we can't use these Data Mining methodologies, what then is the solution? A new methodology called Team Data Science Process (TDSP) may hold some promise.

➜ Team Data Science Process Methodology

TDSP has been developed by Microsoft and is intended for use in data science and with AI project teams.

The Team Data Science Process is, as its name suggests, a methodology for implementing data science projects. It is also applicable for projects that use machine learning or artificial intelligence models. First, let us understand the TDSP lifecycle to see how this may work for your AI project.

The TDSP lifecycle is composed of five stages:

1. Business Understanding

2. Data Acquisition and Understanding

3. Modeling

4. Deployment

5. Customer Acceptance

You'll remember that we outlined a six-step Machine Learning workflow. The first two steps (Problem Definition and Data Preparation) are similar to the first two stages of TDSP. Steps 3 and 4 (Model Development and Performance Tuning) are considered the Modeling stage in TDSP, while steps 5 and 6 (Model Deployment and Model Management) are together referred to as Deployment, which is Stage 4 of TDSP.

There is an additional stage called Customer Acceptance. There are two main tasks of the customer acceptance stage:

→ **System Validation:** Confirming that the deployed solution meets the customer requirements.

→ **Project Hand-off:** Handing the project to the team or group that will be running it in production. This could be an IT or other team of the customer, or even a vendor of the customer that's responsible for running it in production.

TDSP is well-documented, and for each of the five stages, goals, how-tos (specific tasks and guidance), and artifacts (deliverables and sample templates) are available.

TDSP Artifacts

Having understood the various stages of TDSP lifecycle, let us take a step back and examine the different components of the TDSP toolkit.

TDSP consists of

1. A life cycle definition (what we just went through)

2. A standard project structure. This refers to the standard folder directory structure and templates for project documents.

3. Infrastructure for AI projects. Recommendations on technical components such as cloud storage (for storing the datasets), databases and big data clusters, and machine services are provided.

4. Tools and utilities for project execution. Some common tools and reusable scripts for activities such as data exploration and creating shared code repositories are also available.

TDSP also identifies common project roles and the tasks for those roles. Namely, Project Manager, Project Lead, Data Scientist, and Solution Architect. Note that the project roles are going to vary based on the specific project as well as your organizational preferences and norms.

Study it, understand it, and adapt it to your requirements, whichever tool you may be using. Some organizations may even want to build their own version of such a methodology.

Key Points from this chapter:

1. AI skills are in short supply. Consider training your existing team members.

2. AI projects are very different to traditional IT projects and should be run differently.

3. AI projects never really end.

4. You need a Data Scientist for your project–they create and test the Machine Learning model.

5. Business analysts are critical–they need to know your business in-depth.

6. You need a clearly defined and authorized project manager.

7. Divide your AI team into a data group, a machine learning group, and a business group.

8. Some AI teams will be large, some small–but all the roles defined here need to be addressed. There are no shortcuts.

9. Always use a project management methodology–don't just wing it.

10. Consider using the TDSP Methodology developed by Microsoft.

6

AI Technology Selection

It may not come as a surprise to you that there is a very crowded marketplace for AI solutions. On the other hand, we encounter many people who are under the impression that it's all about larger vendors such as IBM, Amazon, Google, and Microsoft. Trust us, it's not—there are thousands of AI technologies available.

That also means that this is a rapidly changing marketplace. There are many small firms: some that will fail, others that will grow into big firms, and many that will be acquired and become part of a larger business. Enterprise AI is in its early days and many, many firms are in the process of coming to the market. There is a lot of hype, which is a polite way of saying there are a lot of firms over-promising and under-delivering. Frankly, many are preying on the buyers who have a lack of knowledge or sophistication.

That leads to a situation we call *AI Washing*; there are a lot of products on the market that claim to be AI products that are no such thing. In some cases, they may leverage some machine learning or analytics, but at the end of the day they are simply adding the term AI to their marketing because they think it will boost sales. They hope that you, the unfortunate buyer, will not know the difference. It's wrong but it's rampant, so caveat emptor or buyer beware!

There is a plethora of tools available, leveraging different methods, frameworks, and approaches. Some are open source, some proprietary, some only run on premises, some in the cloud, some you buy upfront, others you essentially rent via a SaaS (software as a service agreement). There are horizontal AI systems that claim to be a fit for multiple situations, alongside a growing number of specialist AI tools designed for a particular activity or industry process.

Finally, it's important to understand that though some AI tools and areas of activity are pretty robust and mature, others are very immature indeed. You will be their guinea pigs—if you go with such immature tools, you may end up doing their testing for them.

Here's the interesting thing: by working your way through this book, you are more equipped than most to navigate knowledgeably this fast-moving market. We would go further and say that you may well be the best-informed customer a vendor will encounter. You are well-positioned to help your organization make the right AI technology choices. Now you are in the driving seat with all the great knowledge you have taken onboard—which road are you going to take? Let's look at the AI vendors by category that you are likely to encounter.

→ The AI Technology Stack

A useful way to cut through the confusing maze of categories and options is to take a technology stack view. Think of the AI stack as the set of key components and tools required to build a modern AI application.

We can categorize this AI stack into five major categories. Of course, you can categorize them into even more granular levels or slightly differently, but we found this to be a practical but not overly complex way of understanding the stack.

➜ Interactive Tools / IDEs

The first category here is the interactive data science tools. These are used by data scientists to prototype and experiment with machine learning. The major tools available are Jupyter, R studio, and Apache Zeppelin. There are also others such as SeaHorse and OpenRefine.

These are coding applications where you can test code or models, visualize data, etc. The choice of tool will probably come down to the one your data scientists are comfortable with using. There are both open source free and paid-for tools available. You will need one of these for your project, but it should not break the bank. Which one you choose is likely as simple as ensuring it's the one your data scientists like to use.

The IDE tool should support your organization's/data science team's programming language of choice and be suited for the domain of application. Note that machine learning applications can be developed in a variety of programming languages such as Python, C/C++, Java, and R. Here is a quick rundown of which language is being used when.

➜ Programming Languages

➜ Python is a general-purpose programming language with a lot of libraries and extensions for statistics, data processing, machine learning, and deep learning. Because of its versatility, Python is currently the most popular language for building machine learning applications. Among others, Python is a popular choice for natural language processing, sentiment analysis, and web data mining applications.

- C/C++ is popular among developers of AI applications for games, physical robot control, and cybersecurity.

- Java is being used for AI applications around cybersecurity, fraud detection, and customer support.

- R is a programming language for statistical computing. Among others, it is extensively used in AI applications for bioinformatics and bioengineering.

→ Machine Learning Frameworks

Next, let's look at machine learning frameworks. The frameworks or libraries encapsulate the implementations of several machine learning algorithms and models, including deep learning models. These are exciting because usually the innovations and breakthroughs in the field of machine learning are first implemented as new frameworks or libraries. Many of the frameworks that you see have been first implemented by a leading technology firm such as a Google or a Facebook, then released to the broader community of practitioners, and eventually make their way into commercial products.

Most of these frameworks also support multiple languages like C++, Python, R, or server-side JavaScript. These are developer-friendly environments, easy to code on, and provide you with a library of pre-built components to help you build your system. They also typically connect you to a community of other developers to share code and components.

- TensforFlow is a very popular deep learning framework. This framework was initially developed by Google, found extensive use internally within Google, and has since been open sourced.

- Caffe was originally developed by the Berkeley Group, and Caffe2 has been extended and used by Facebook.
- CNTK is an open source deep learning framework that has been developed by Microsoft.
- Scikit-learn is based on Python. Prior to the release of TensorFlow it was the most popular machine learning framework.
- Keras provides a user-friendly interface to TensorFlow and CNTK and allows for quick prototyping and development.
- MXNet is a deep learning framework by Amazon.
- Gluon is an API developed by Microsoft and Amazon. It supports MXNet, CNTKm and other frameworks. It offers easy building blocks for neural networks and comes as a part of MXNet.
- Theano is a Python library to efficiently compute matrix operations.
- Pytorch: Torch is a library for deep learning and needs a programming language called Lua. Pytorch is a similar framework that uses Python. It has been developed and used by Facebook.
- Paddle Paddle is a deep learning framework originally developed by Chinese technology company Baidu.
- Apache Flink is a tool used for real-time data processing applications.
- SparkML is a machine learning library from Apache.

Yes, that's a lot of libraries and frameworks to take in. Just remember that these are the interfaces or tools where you will actually build your production machine learning models. The capabilities of these libraries and frameworks are updated quite rapidly and new frameworks keep getting released. The takeaway for you is that these libraries contain the actual code that implements the machine learning algorithms that your data science team leverages.

➜ COTS / ML APIs

A lot of the frameworks that you saw in the last section (such as TensorFlow and Pytorch) are open source. To leverage them, you need access to expert resources who are well-versed in those frameworks. Because the frameworks are relatively new (and because of the overall shortage of such talent), that's not always the case.

The commercial products that you see package many machine learning capabilities into an easy-to-use software product. Many of them also offer some pre-trained models. The advantage is that you can get started fairly quickly and you have the support of vendor who sells you the software. The flipside is, of course, the license and usage costs.

Google, IBM, Amazon, and Microsoft provide these machine learning capabilities as APIs (e.g. speech processing, language processing, image recognition) that can be easily invoked and consumed from other applications.

Products such as Algorithmia, H2O.ai, Dataiku, Rapid Miner, and Knime offer packaged products for machine learning application development from data preparation to model deployment, or sometimes even model management. You need to consider the type of models that they support. For instance, not all of them support the deep learning functionality that you saw in the open source frameworks previously. They also have their areas of strengths and weaknesses. Algorithmia provides search and categorization options and libraries of pre-built algorithms. KNIME has a reputation as being very intuitive and easy-to-use. Rapidminer prides itself in delivering predictive analytics models, etc.

With machine learning APIs and products, you will have a lot of choice. What you are basically buying here are ready-to-use capabilities in a highly usable form that can get you started with AI very quickly. There are many options to choose from. Do your homework and compare and contrast to fit your specific needs and use cases.

➡ Runtime/Infrastructure

Now we will get into the infrastructure, as we are looking at the category of runtime/infrastructure platforms. These platforms help train and run machine learning models. To train and run high-performance machine learning models at-scale, you need a lot of storage and compute resources. Specialized servers that use GPUs can speed up model training times (and when you develop models iteratively, you'll want to train models as efficiently as possible). Of course, there is a trade-off here between cost and performance.

Again, you see the major names like Amazon at play here, essentially offering AI runtime architecture as a service. But there are other options such as H2O.ai or Domino or Databricks for you to consider. The choice of the infrastructure is also dependent on the application characteristics.

➡ Clouds

You can say that while Open Source machine learning frameworks are democratizing machine learning, machine learning clouds are making it easier than ever before for companies to get started with machine learning applications.

For this reason, some buyers gravitate quickly to machine learning clouds. This category is dominated by Amazon, Google, IBM and Microsoft—note that these are also the leaders in traditional cloud platforms. Due to the sheer scale of these vendors, they are able to offer full platform environments that cover off the majority of application area often with end-to-end functionality. They also have the deep pockets to drive rapid innovation and add new features to their clouds.

It may seem like a no-brainer to take the machine learning cloud route, and for some it is. But there are drawbacks to this approach. For example, like a lot of cloud services, they can start out cheap and end up being very expensive.

Another consideration is where you want your AI to sit. If it needs to be integrated in an existing application, leveraging a cloud service may not be the right option. Again, there are trade-offs involved.

➡ Build versus Buy

Looking at the categories, you can see that the line between build versus buy is often quite blurred. So, let's explore that a little further...

When deciding whether to build your own AI or simply buy one you will need to consider these factors carefully.

1. What is your existing IT stack? Is it capable of handling AI? Are you going to be using AI to augment existing processes and

activities and does that mean you need to integrate the AI into a business application?

2. Do you have the skill sets to build your own AI? These are not easy to come by, but if you have them or can get them, then building your own may be an option.

We have advised on many buying decisions over the years and have learned the hard way how important your internal culture and vendor relationships are to this kind of decision. Some organizations like to build their own tech while others don't, simple as that. That is often a barrier that cannot be overcome no matter what logic you use to argue the opposite. But the one that is often underappreciated is the relationship you have with vendors. Good technology and a great relationship with your vendor/supplier are often a better option than awesome technology and a weak relationship. AI projects are complex, you need to be comfortable and have trust in one another when working together.

Lastly, you need to decide if it's worth the effort to build your own if there is an off-the-shelf alternative that is a great fit already.

Whether you build or buy, whether you want to run in the cloud or on premises, use proprietary technology or go open source, there is no shortage of options. The choice is yours.

As an illustration, let's look at the choices you have if you are considering an NLP project.

→ Leverage Cloud Platforms: (e.g. Amazon AWS Lex or Microsoft Luis)

→ Buy from Specialist vendors: (e.g. Kore.AI, BotCore)

→ Build on top of open source (e.g. SpaCY, Stanford NLP)

Likewise, if you are considering an Optical Character Recognition (OCR) project, your choices are many -- Cloud (e.g. AWS Rekognition), COTS (e.g. ABBYY), Open Source (e.g. Tesseract).

There are examples of companies having pursued any one of these options depending on their project requirements, organizational context, budgetary constraints, and their overall enterprise technology standards and stacks.

The core message is that you have several options and you need to look into them carefully to pick the one that meets your requirements.

Though in reality it's not *quite* as simple as this, the fact of the matter is that if you build your own AI you will have greater control over it and have the opportunity to really differentiate your operation. Of course, how well you do will depend on the skills you have in-house to do the work.

Similarly, if you buy a packaged AI then it should be good enough for your needs, but it's unlikely to be optimized and it won't differentiate you. It's the same thing everyone else is using.

You may simply outsource all your AI work if you don't have the skills and don't want to leverage packaged applications, but control will be lost in the process no matter how carefully you manage the engagement. For many, the decision to build or buy will not be that clear-cut—you will build what is critical for you to control and differentiate, and use packaged apps for rest of the work.

→ Making the Right Technology Selection

Even with limited time and resources, you need to consider your options carefully. The wrong technology decision can completely derail your project or set you back by a few quarters or even years. Trust us—we've seen it happen. You also need to consider the fast-changing landscape and ensure you don't get locked into the wrong options and can't get out. That's the same for most enterprise technology selection decisions, but as you have learned in this book, once up and running for a period of time it's hard to switch AI off or change your options.

Let us offer you some best practices or thumb rules that we've seen to be pretty successful.

Firstly, AI systems have to work together with your existing technology and software. Your organization may already have some existing data science platforms (particularly if you have been implementing some big data or analytics applications). You can use that to get started and develop some prototypes and pilots. The advantage is that your team will already be familiar with the tools and there need be no delays on procurement, getting approvals from enterprise architecture standards teams, etc.

Next, look for pre-trained models that are available for your use case. Such models are available by industry (e.g. credit risk scoring), by function (e.g. lead scoring for marketing), or by process (customer churn prediction). Often, they can give you a jumpstart or make up for lack of deep data science talent.

Cloud APIs are getting more extensive, and we can expect that trend to continue. Depending on the architecture of your line-of-business applications (i.e. if it is easy to consume 3rd party APIs), you may be able to leverage the AI-capabilities from within them directly. As we discussed, look within the open source libraries and deep learning frameworks. This is really the place where the latest and greatest in machine learning capabilities are getting released first.

Even the most sophisticated technology needs to be paired with industry/domain knowledge. No one knows your business as well as you do. For your AI projects to be successful, you need to find vendors and products that can demonstrate domain expertise and have resources that understand the issues of your industry.

Now, let's turn our attention to the detailed due diligence that you want to conduct during the AI technology selection process.

→ Technology Due Diligence

Needless to say, you'll evaluate the core AI capabilities (e.g. image or natural language processing services) and the Total Cost of Ownership aspects (pricing and other commercial details). But beyond that, you need to look at a set of interrelated factors such as data management, model development, model management, and enterprise standards.

First, let us look at Data Management related aspects. Evaluate the data preparation capabilities of the product. Can you enrich and extend existing data with external data sources? Can you aggregate and decompose data easily?

Evaluate the breadth of database connectivity. Does it connect to traditional SQL data stores, newer data sources (e.g. NoSQL), and also cloud repositories? Can you visually explore data, understand the data characteristics, and drill down into the data?

Next, consider the machine learning modeling related functionality. Does it support the programming languages your team is considering using? Does it support the algorithms that are necessary for your use cases? What kind of feature selection and feature engineering capabilities does the product support?

How easy to setup and use is the development environment? What is the extent of support for collaborative and distributed code development?

Remember that your teams will be spending a lot (if not the bulk) of their time in the data preparation, iterative model building, feature selection, and model tuning. The product should make these activities easy and improve their productivity.

Also evaluate the product capabilities when it comes to model management post-deployment. We find that these activities are highly manual in many organizations, and you should prefer a product that can automate as many of the "pipeline" activities as possible. Check whether the product supports automatic versioning and rollback of models and data deployed in production. What kind of performance monitoring services does the product support?

Also, don't forget the risks and biases that we cover in great length later on in this book. Refer to the Trusted AI Checklist that addresses the issue of bias in AI systems and datasets.

Last but not least, look at the usability features, scalability aspects, collaboration features, and integration functionality the product offers. These are the factors you consider when you evaluate any enterprise software product, not just AI. Additionally, for AI products, you have to evaluate auditability–can you log and trace the system's actions?

Don't buy anything before you are satisfied that the product meets your requirement boxes along these dimensions. You may not find a tool that meets all your requirements, and will need to work around a few shortcomings, but know those beforehand rather than when it's too late to avoid post-purchase regret.

It may be advisable to get some expert outside help when going through the selection and evaluation process, but whether you do or not, ensure you run a thorough due diligence process every time.

Everything in this chapter (and indeed the entire book) has been drawn from real world AI enterprise experiences and projects. It's not just theoretical, it's practical and tried-and-tested. By following the advice we have given, you'll significantly increase your chances of success.

Key Points from this chapter:

1. The marketplace for AI is crowded. It is not just about Google, Amazon, IBM, and Microsoft; there are many more options.

2. Beware of AI Washing. Not everything labelled as AI really is.

3. The AI technology stack consists of Cloud Platforms, Specialist COTS, Developer Tools, Machine Learning Frameworks, and Infrastructure.

4. You can build or buy AI–the lines between each are blurred.

5. You need to consider your options carefully. The wrong

selection can doom your project.

6. Do proper due diligence on any product you select.

7. Carefully evaluate the data preparation capabilities of any product you consider.

8. Be aware that your team will spend most of its time on data preparation.

9. Consider getting outside (independent) help in the early stages of your AI project.

10. Consider usability carefully–the smartest system is of little use if it is hard or impossible to use.

7

The Dark Side
of AI

Understanding biases and blind spots in AI is an incredibly important topic, but as you will see it's not something that is understood or discussed often enough, or in enough depth. To put it bluntly, AI has a dark side and this is not something that technology vendors or consultants want to talk about. In some cases, the dark side of AI is not something they fully appreciate the importance of. As a reader of this book, we assume you are looking to use AI and ML in your organization, and you need to be fully aware of the potential problems and appreciate the importance of dealing with them, as it will be you that is left holding the can if things go wrong.

Before and during any AI project or planning exercise, you need to seriously consider any issues of bias and blind spots in your AI.

In this chapter, as you will have already guessed, we look at this different and very important side of AI. While the promise and potential of AI is certainly exciting, and the press is full of stories marveling at its power, there are reasons to worry. There are risks that we need to acknowledge and prepare for in our embrace of AI.

To be clear from the start, we are passionate supporters and advocates for the use of AI in business, but we are also pragmatists.

Anything that promises so much must be treated with caution—and AI promises the world. Once you seriously embark down the road with AI, it can be difficult to turn back. So, before you start, we need to point out some of the pitfalls you might encounter and provide you with a roadmap and some guidance to deal with those situations when they occur.

Much of what we share in this chapter will seem fuzzy and subjective. Oddly enough, that is the point. AI is not as clear-cut, accurate, or unbiased in its work as its creators lead us to believe. As many of us were taught as children, you must "Be prepared!" By the conclusion of this chapter, you will at least be well informed, and hopefully prepared for the interesting and sometimes bumpy journey in AI that you have ahead of you.

If there is one thing that we can all agree on, it's that while AI has in the past few years become more powerful and more capable than ever before, it's still a maturing area. Yes, AI has been around a long time, but as we have seen it's only recently that it has really started to take center stage to the point that everyone who is online today is interacting with AI in one form or another. AI is popping up everywhere, you interact with it daily—but haven't you experienced a few situations when the AI system seemed to be off a bit?

Think about online advertisements that seem to think for one reason or another that you are in the market to buy Kanye West's new album, a new Toyota SUV, or a timeshare in Barbados. Advertisers think this is what you want, but you really don't. Or maybe there are times when you are searching online for something that you know for sure is there, but you can't seem to find it. Something in the AI system isn't quite delivering the results it should. We can live with this situation, it's not really a big deal in these situations, at best it's a bit annoying.

Eventually, you will find the information that you are searching for, you are not going to buy Kanye's new album, no matter how many times you are prompted, and life goes on. You may even conclude that over time the AI will get better and those problems will go away.

Obviously, in these cases there is the possible downside of a loss of productivity and efficiency, and in some cases even some frustration—all undesirable consequences. But they happen regularly, we move on with our lives and work, and we don't give them too much attention, nor should we. But the root causes of these issues, these mistakes, can also lead to more serious situations and negative consequences when AI misfires.

→ Microsoft Gets AI Wrong

The story of Microsoft's ill-fated "Tay" system is one of the most documented AI failures of recent years, but it's so dramatic that it's worth revisiting.

Launched in March 2016, the goal of this AI bot was to mimic the conversational style of a 19-year-old woman. It was supposed to be playful and casual in conversational interactions with humans on platforms such as Twitter. Tay was designed to bring a touch of fun into human bot conversations. The ultimate goal of Tay was to engage, entertain, and ultimately for Microsoft to better understand the real world of culture and conversations for people in their late teens and early twenties.

Tay was, by any measure, a complete and utter disaster. Sixteen hours after it was launched, Tay was shut down. In that short period of time, it had become a conversational bot that was deeply racist and sexist, one that supported wild conspiracy theories and was downright genocidal. Tay's launch could not have gone worse.

To put this into some context, Tay was a chat bot developed by a firm with near-unlimited resources at its disposal. Microsoft has access to truly massive data sets and computing power. Tay was developed by the crème de la crème of AI experts. Tay was tested thoroughly before its release. Despite all of these advantages, Tay was a spectacular failure.

So, what the heck went wrong? Clearly many things went wrong, but at the most fundamental level, like any AI or Machine Learning tool, Tay was only really able to recognize patterns. It could never hope to truly understand the meaning of words in human conversations in an ever changing world, let alone understand their full impact or context.

Scientists and mathematicians want to believe the world is pure logic, that everything can be reduced to an equation. But when AI interacts with real people in the real world, things are seldom right or wrong, black or white. More often, they are infinitely nuanced and complex. Tay reacted to what it saw and responded accordingly; it saw patterns and drew conclusions. Tay did not work incorrectly. It did what it was told to do. All too often, AI developers intentionally ignore the negative aspects, as they have faith that the AI will learn what we want it to learn. But in the real world of human dynamics, that is not always possible. To repeat again from our section on neural networks, AI does not work the same way as the human brain, it simply mimics some basic functions. AI has no moral compass. It does not think or feel. It simply recognizes patterns and responds.

A key takeaway here is that AI systems are not just tools. In many different and increasingly complex ways, they directly interact with us humans, with society. AI can shape our actions, decisions, and behavior. AI tools don't know right from wrong, good from bad. Our best efforts of programming ethics and moral compasses into AI are likely to fall short. In real life there are few absolutes regarding what is wrong and right. What is correct and justifiable to one person or one community may be offensive or even harmful to another. One only has to switch on the news to see how that plays out.

Microsoft Tay is a great case study in AI-human interactions. The lessons of Tay are not all negative, we can (and have) learned a lot from those 16 hours online, lessons that have applicability far beyond Twitter and chat bots.

→ Google Photos

Another prime-time example of AI going wrong was when Google Photos was found to have mislabeled a woman of color as a gorilla. This is, of course, deeply offensive. Google went as far as to offer a seemingly very genuine apology for the mistake saying that they were "appalled and genuinely sorry." First Google said they would correct the algorithm, then went a step further and then simply removed offending labels related to primates. Even though this incident was first reported in 2015, a test in 2018 by *Wired* Magazine showed no real progress had been made in fixing this situation other than censoring terms related to certain primates.

This awful example of AI misfiring is an illustration of the fact that AI tools only know what they know. Their world view, if we can call it that, is based entirely on the world they have been shown through data. Many AI facial recognition and language recognition systems are far more accurate when analyzing white faces and the English language than they are at anything else, because that is what they know best.

Practical Artificial Intelligence | *An Enterprise Playbook*

They represent the bulk of the data they have been exposed to. When presented with non-white faces or less familiar languages, they perform much less well as they have been exposed to much less relevant data. The same would be true in reverse of an AI system developed in China using Chinese data.

If you are anything like us, your toes will have curled at this example, as it's a shockingly unpleasant instance of AI getting things wrong, but it's an important one to consider as such mistakes and the reason they occur have much broader implications beyond the use of Google Photos.

→ Fatal Car Crash

If the last two examples weren't bad enough, now we have an example of an AI-driven vehicle involved in a fatal crash. This wasn't the only crash; there have been many such accidents, though to date, fortunately, few have been fatal.

Let's put a context around this example—the premise is quite simple. Fully autonomous AI-driven cars should be safer on the roads than human-driven cars, but that doesn't mean they don't and won't make mistakes. Anyone who drives a car, be it in the country or in the city, knows that driving can be very unpredictable. As a driver you are trained to expect the unexpected, but even so, stuff happens.

In 2018, an Uber self-driving car killed a woman in Tempe, Arizona during a test. This incident brought to a standstill several autonomous vehicle tests and trials (though not for long, it might be noted). The car was traveling on a dimly lit road when a woman pushing a bicycle came out of the darkness. The car was driving at 40 mph (64 kmph),, and the result was a fatal crash. In theory, at least, it simply should not have happened, but it did. Uber employees had warned those in charge of the test that such an incident may occur.

In the Uber crash here, we might consider that it's possible that the image recognition system was simply confused by a pedestrian walking a bicycle. If that was the case then it can be corrected, but can an autonomous vehicle really ever learn all the vagaries of driving a car in the real world, on ever changing infrastructure, with real humans in the equation? The answer is that we don't know. The theory goes that autonomous AI-driven vehicles will get better and better as they learn. But there is an equally strong counter-argument, that says surprising and unpredictable events occur in driving situations all the time and a generalized approach of AI learning may never truly crack the code. Life is messy, stuff happens, and not everything can be predicted.

→ AI Makes Mistakes

Hopefully we have shaken you up a bit and have your undivided attention. Our point is simple: AI is not perfect, it makes mistakes, and those mistakes can have real world consequences. Sometimes those mistakes just add a bit of annoyance to our already busy lives, sometimes the consequences are severe. Let's take this a step further and focus on a tricky and difficult area for AI: gender detection using images.

The process is pretty straightforward. We ask the AI system to detect if there is a face in an image. If there is, then we may do one of two general things in our analysis. We may try to exactly match that face with another face we have stored in our system. Think, for example, of using an exact match of your face to unlock your phone or to enable you to pay for something at a kiosk based on the system recognizing that you are really you. We are identifying or verifying that you are really you.

In other situations, we want to do some classification work regarding what a face image tells us about this particular person. For example, how old are they, is this a man or woman, or what kind of emotion are they displaying?

To the human eye and brain, it is relatively easy to identify, verify, or classify based solely on a brief glimpse of a person's face. Yet for AI, these kinds of tasks can prove to be very difficult to do within an acceptable degree of accuracy. Remember, when the AI system gets it wrong, there can be consequences.

Image Recognition Datasets

As we know, AI-driven machines can look at a lot of data, they can defeat world chess champions and safely drive cars—well, most of the time at least. In a study, MIT researchers compared the accuracy of three major AI tools that were designed for facial recognition classifications, side-by-side. The tools they compared were from IBM, Microsoft, and a company called Faceplusplus from China. The researchers built a strong and seemingly balanced data set, but in the test, they found that white men and women and men of color were more accurately detected than women of color.

Why this disparity? Many data sets are severely flawed by imbalance; many data sets have far more images of white males than any other group. What this meant was that even when the MIT team used a truly balanced set of images in their analysis, the tools still didn't perform well, as they had all likely been trained on imbalanced data sets.

This gets us into difficult territory that is far beyond the scope of this book, but the fact is that the imbalances we encounter in the real world can and often are represented in the data sets used to train AI. This results in the AI system having an equally unbalanced view of the world as we do.

Even in a huge data set, there may be only a small number of pieces of data that veer from the norm. So, the system will have lots of data to consider for the average norm (in this case, white people), but far less to learn about more marginalized groups. Consider that in the context of the classification of a facial image: big bucket categories like Black, White, or Asian are very blunt instruments in a world of regional and ethnic groups and subgroups.

→ Can we ever have fair and balanced AI?

As we have seen when the human and the computer worlds collide, mistakes can be made. Oftentimes these mistakes are based on errors or an imbalance in the data that is analyzed, or that the AI system trains on. Ultimately, we want our AI systems to be unbiased. We want them to make fair decisions. True fairness is very hard to achieve in AI, and some may argue that it is virtually impossible.

In the world of AI there is an active discussion regarding fairness and bias, and we encourage you to explore and get involved in these discussions. What you will find is that the issue of bias and fairness in AI is not only a complex and controversial area of discussion, but it's also one that is only recently going mainstream, one that we should have had years ago but sadly we are only starting to debate now.

When an algorithm is not fair, it can impact both individuals and society as a whole. It can enforce rather than reduce discriminations such as sexism, ageism, or racism. It can give us a skewed notion of accuracy in matters of criminal justice. It can even help, and is in fact often used deliberately, to promote fake news, images, and videos.

Let's look at a few more examples of AI out in the real world. There is an AI system called COMPAS that is widely used in the US to predict the likelihood of a defendant re-offending. COMPAS and other systems like it are also used to determine sentencing, release, and crime hotspots. In US states such as Arizona, Colorado, and Kentucky, COMPAS is used to provide a risk assessment of a defendant's likelihood of reoffending. The results of this assessment are given to judges during criminal sentencing.

Does it work? That's arguable, all we know for sure is that it is used every day in the US justice system. We also know that it has produced many curious–at times bizarre–decisions, to the point that in 2014 the then Attorney General called for the US Sentencing Commission to investigate its use and effectiveness. They didn't do that, but in tests run independently by ProPublica, it turned out that COMPAS performed no better than random humans taken from the street when given the same–or in some cases less–information. The point is that COMPAS and any systems like it are not blind to bias, nor are they likely to be any fairer in their decision-making than humans.

Amazon also experimented with the use of AI to help in its human decision-making processes to ensure more fairness in its recruitment practice. However, it turned out that the new AI system was just as sexist and discriminatory as the same process conducted by humans. Why? Well it seems (you may be spotting a pattern here!) that the system learned by reviewing past resumes that were predominantly male. In short, it taught itself to be sexist. In fact, it was trained on ten years of resumes that the company had received, but as the tech sector is male-dominated, the majority of those resumes came from men. Even after trying to fix some of the issues, Amazon ultimately decided to pull the plug as all they could really do was fix obvious biases, such as the system downgrading graduates of women's colleges; the patterns ran much deeper in the data, and Amazon could not be sure that it had fixed it.

Never assume that AI is inherently unbiased, that somehow because it is a machine it comes to situations with a clean and fair mindset. All AI and ML needs to be trained, and the bias in the data they use to train means the underlying algorithms also become biased. Finally, let's take note that like the Microsoft Tay example we used earlier, Amazon is a firm with the best of the best technology with near unlimited resources, yet even they got something like this terribly wrong.

Up until now we have talked about systems that made (arguably) innocent mistakes. But the manner in how those mistakes were made can be exploited by bad actors to identify and discriminate against groups of people they don't like. In fact, such deliberate manipulation of data has already started (e.g. automatically generate propaganda on social media). Today we have the reality of what are called generative adversarial networks, where AI is being used to generate realistic fake images and videos for political purposes. Fake news, regardless of your political stance, is a reality and it is not simply a case of people claiming something they don't like is by default "fake." News is being generated deliberately to mislead, thanks to the wonders of AI.

➔ Harms of Algorithmic Bias

It is easy to think that the issues we just explored of deliberate and accidental discriminations and bias are not pertinent to the real world most of us live in. In reality, they impact many areas of our work and personal lives. We need to be aware of these problems before we start any project, and be aware that no matter how good our data set is, it includes biases that we may identify with or be impacted by, but may not be able to easily detect.

➔ Transparent and Trusted AI?

In this next section, we are going to look at issues related to trust and transparency in AI. If we understand that bias and blind spots are always going to exist in AI, how can we spot and address them?

1. The first thing we must do is to use training data that is as free of bias as we can manage, to ensure some level of fairness. The likelihood is that your data does include bias, but then again not all data sets are equal. Some sets will be much less weighted by bias than others. You need to carefully consider the source and quality of the data you use to train your AI. You also need to be realistic about what it may and may not contain. Finally, you need to understand that more data is not necessarily better data. Quality trumps quantity every time.

2. Think about how you will use your AI, what its purposes and goals are, and ensure you carefully select the right data for your specific purposes. This may seem obvious, but in the world of AI there are many data sets available to you both inside and external to your organization. The mantra up until now has been "The more the data, the better the data" but select carefully, go for high quality,

and select with your eyes open to any hidden bias.

3. Your system needs to be robust and needs to work well, but it goes beyond that. You need to ensure that your system cannot be tampered with nor can your training data be compromised. One seemingly minor trip up can cause a huge amount of damage. Spot the cause of damage before it could be too late.

4. Your AI needs to be explainable. You need to be able to interpret `its results and understand how it came to its decisions, particularly controversial or contentious decisions. If you can't explain how it comes to its decisions and your AI starts making wrong decisions, your only option may be to shut it down.

5. Finally, there is the concept of lineage—in other words, all the details of how the system was developed, deployed, and maintained and kept easily available for auditing.

Together, these four principles represent the core of any trusted AI system. In short, you need the **right data**, a **secure system** that is **explainable**, and one that has a **well-documented lineage**.

→ Performance vs. Transparency

As you have learned in the previous chapters, there are different structures and approaches to AI, from relatively simple decision trees to highly sophisticated neural networks. Each method has its relative strengths and weaknesses. Each can be used selectively to meet your specific AI needs. But for many situations, you need to be able to explain how your AI made a decision. The process of decision making by AI needs to be transparent.

When we come to transparency in AI there is a tradeoff to be made between performance and explainability. Neural networks deliver high performance and can undertake the most complex of tasks and analysis, but conversely, they are also by far the most difficult to unravel and explain how they made their decisions. Realistically, many neural networks are impossible for a human to unravel and explain. Neural networks are by default black boxes that cannot be explained. You need to be aware of that and take that into account when choosing your approach and methods.

But of course, it's not as simple as that. Let's be honest: nothing in the AI world is simple! There is a secondary tradeoff to be made. If you have an open and explainable AI system, then you are also *potentially* providing an opportunity for bad actors to reverse engineer the model. In fact, some experts go further and suggest that explainable AI may actually make our systems weaker. Maybe that is true, maybe it's not—as with so many of these cases, it all depends on what you do with your AI and how you manage it over time. You do need to be aware of the potential tradeoffs between explainable and black box AI approaches and choose wisely.

→ Why Explainable AI?

Let's expand this argument with ourselves a bit further. If explainable AI potentially means weaker AI, then why might we want our AI system to be explainable? One of the key reasons is that more and more regulatory requirements now, and in the future, may demand it. These include regulations like the Equal Credit Opportunity Act in the US or the EU's Right to Explanation Act.

Both these and many other regulations want to ensure against discrimination and give an opportunity to explain why difficult decisions were made. They also want to ensure there is the right to address and resolve any bad decisions.

To put it another way, if you were to be accused of violating regulations, then you need to prove that you were not in fact violating the regulation. If you can't explain how your AI makes its decisions, then you could be in a bit of a pickle. This is something to consider carefully when making your choice of AI.

Another reason for explainability is to gain executive sponsorship and support for your AI work. Quite understandably, executives are always going to be more likely to agree to the recommendations and decisions produced by an AI system if they can be explained in business language that they understand.

Finally, you need to consider the fact that any AI system is going to need to change and adapt over time. You will want to improve the models, and address or avoid problems like spurious correlations (i.e. imagining relationships and patterns where none exist). Similarly, you may want to bring new domain knowledge to your model building. If you don't know how the model is constructed and operates today, how will you modify it in the future? This is a series of tradeoffs that you need to be aware of and deal with in your AI work.

But coming up is another tug of war that you will encounter. Did you guess what the tug of war was? It's the seemingly eternal battle between IT and the business, or as we label it, the AI creators and the AI enablers. The tussle between the data scientists and business analysts. When it comes to whether AI should be explainable or not, you have two groups with often radically divergent views.

AI engineers (creators) today may in general make little effort to make AI explainable, as this doesn't help the engineer. The creators will probably have to give up performance gains or document their work more accurately—not something they have ever been keen on.

Conversely, explainability helps the users (enablers) of AI, as it allows them to explain the model to third parties, identify blind spots, and generally ensure everything is working well and in compliance.

Think about how this may play out in your AI project. Think about how you will implement AI, what tools and approaches you may take, and how you will balance the (valid yet) dueling positions of the builders and the users when it comes to explainability.

➡ Trusted AI

If you have come away with one thing from this chapter so far, it is that you need a trusted AI. Let's be honest: an untrusted one sounds terrible and could be disastrous for your business. There are various different models and checklists for building a trusted AI system. Many of them pretty similar to one another, and all are worthy of your consideration. In some regards, they are all common-sense models. Here is our checklist:

- **Define:** Before doing anything, define specifically what your AI service is going to be used for and what output it will produce. An AI for document capture is going to look very different indeed to one designed for HR or Marketing. Be specific. Know your purpose and expected outcomes from the get-go.

- **Expert Advice:** Get a bit more technical. Get expert advice and draw upon the knowledge you have gained from this book. What specific algorithms or techniques will this service implement, use, and require? Remember there are many different approaches, and each has their strengths and weaknesses. Choose wisely.

- **Explainable:** Once you know the intended use and outputs and the techniques, you will use ask yourself whether the outputs will be explainable. In some cases, it may not matter too much, while in others it will be essential that the outputs are explainable, particularly if there is any applicable regulation. You must address this question at the start of your project.

→ **Bias:** This one is clearly going to be a bit subjective and differ according to your needs, but it's important to understand before you start what possible examples of bias might arise and need to be addressed. You also need to consider any ethical, regulatory, and safety risks that might result from using the AI service. AI systems can undertake some very impressive workloads and tasks, but you need to define where the boundaries are, and when and where they cannot be crossed.

→ **Testing:** Testing in AI is, as we have already learned, critical to its success or failure. Which datasets will the AI service be tested on? What methodologies will you use? How will you describe the test results? AI systems learn over time, which means they will not get everything right the first time. Testing and learning from tests are key. Finally, for each dataset the service uses, you need to be sure that it was checked for bias. You need to make a sincere effort to ensure that the data is fair and representative. Remember, nothing is likely to be perfect, so be sure to plan to perform bias detection and have the tools and processes to remediate any situation that arises.

This checklist may not be perfect, but it's a good place to start. We strongly recommend that you follow it closely.

→ Tools for Bias Check

Tools that help you check for bias in your AI data and its processes are becoming available. But note that they are limited in scope, and we are hoping that the tools will mature and become more powerful in the future.

One of the better known tools is one called AI Fairness 360 from IBM. In essence, it is a toolkit of Python programs that can check for bias in data sets and algorithms during the data preparation, data training, and model deployment stages.

But remember that this is just one tool, and it will only be applicable for some use cases. Companies such as Microsoft, Facebook, Google, and Accenture all have already released or announced plans to release similar tools.

Keep your eyes peeled for more coming to the market. Research and test thoroughly before using, as by this point you no doubt understand the importance of bias detection.

→ Is Bias-free AI Even Possible?

The goal is always to create perfect AI, but that's a lofty and unrealistic goal as it will always involve a balancing act between performance and accuracy. But when the right approaches are taken, we can achieve very good AI. Again, what is good is going to be subjective, but the question we really need to ask is: how good does our AI need to be? Take the case of autonomous cars; the starting point was "safer than humans," but after multiple crashes, that bar has been raised. That goalpost will may well continue to move over the coming years.

To achieve good AI, we need an understanding of how the models work, how they make decisions, how those models might change, and how decisions may become more critical over time. We need to understand our data, its quality, and the biases it contains.

We need to realistically accept that despite their lack of transparency, black box models (such as neural networks i.e. deep learning) will continue to be used because of their superior performance and predictive power.

Bias-free AI is theoretically possible because we can consciously examine the bias in the underlying data sets and consider the ethical dimensions of the systems we are building. Having a diverse team (e.g. don't staff your AI team with only software engineers) can also help identify unconscious embedded biases in the systems we build. But theory and practice are two different things; we must make our best efforts, but hidden biases may still have an impact in even the most transparent situations.

→ How Many Biases Can There Really Be?

We all have many biases—even the most radically accepting people in the world have biases. We are complex things, human beings. We don't list them here, but researchers have compiled a list of 180 cognitive human biases. Biases are not limited to gender, race, and age and biases are not always obvious. Sexism, ageism, and racism may seem fairly obvious, but we know from our own lives that even when they are present, they are not always obvious.

➜ A Lesson from the Past

As we are now getting close to wrapping up this book, we wanted to share with you a story about hidden bias that goes back to 1952 and the Boston Symphony Orchestra (BSO). It may sound odd, but what the orchestra experienced then was prescient, instructive, and illuminating for our study of hidden bias in AI.

➜ De-biasing: Boston Symphony Orchestra

Let's go way, way back to 1952.

The BSO knew that they recruited more men than women, but were not sure why, as they prided themselves on only recruiting the best musicians regardless of gender. They wanted to know if their recruitment process was biased.

They took the unusual course of constructing a literal blind test–a physical screen behind which musicians would audition, and the BSO staff would not be able to see if they were male or female.

The theory was that the best musicians, regardless of their gender, would be selected bias-free. It was a good theory, but as we have explored many times in this book, theory and practice don't always match up.

You guessed it, the unexpected happened. Rather than there being a better balance between the genders after this blind audition, things stayed pretty much the same. The BSO started to ask themselves if men really were better musicians than women; it was certainly starting to look that way. But then, somebody had a very smart idea...

They asked the auditioning musicians to take their shoes off before walking on stage, and something magical occurred.

Suddenly, far more women were successful in the auditions. There was almost an equal 50-50 split between men and women selected! It was the sound of the shoes that gave away the gender.

There was a bias, but arguably it was an unconscious one. These were people trying to do the "right thing," but there was a discriminatory bias nonetheless that was eventually revealed, and they went some way to remedying it. Pretty impressive, right?

AI systems, just like humans, are not perfect. AI needs knowledgeable and skilled help to guide it. We need more skilled people to get involved and to be a part of the AI revolution to help steer it in the right direction. We hope that you are one of those future leaders, and that we have given you much to consider and to help you get started on the journey.

You may be thinking to yourself that there are more questions to ask than answers to give. That is exactly as it should be. AI is not dark, nor is it light; rather, it is reflective of what it sees. It's your job to ensure it is seeing the right things in the right way.

Key Points in this chapter:

1. Before starting any AI project you need to carefully consider biases and blind spots in your AI.

2. Biases are real, and there are many of them both conscious and unconscious, simple and complicated.

3. AI is not as clear-cut, accurate, or unbiased as its creators would lead us to believe.

4. Even major firms like Microsoft and Google can get AI badly wrong.

5. AI tools don't know good from bad or right from wrong.

6. Ultimately everything is biased, that is what context is.

7. One person's view of a situation will differ from another's. One group in society will view things differently to another group; those views reflect bias. That is no different in AI.

8. We can potentially work with AI to reduce and nullify some biases.

9. AI can equally be used to accentuate existing biases or even add new biases to the equation.

10. AI systems are not just tools, they can shape our actions, decisions and behaviors. Tread carefully

Final Thoughts

This is a short book, but we have covered a lot of ground. Our goal was to ensure we covered the most important things: the things you really need to know to get started with AI, the things that will help you to be successful. We have tried our best to keep this practical, and to make the core technology elements as digestible as possible. But this is just the start. There is a wealth of resources out there for you to explore and plunder, to dig deeper and to learn more. Even if this is the only book you read, we hope you go away with a fundamental grasp of the most important elements of any AI project. Let's summarize these key elements right now.

→ Getting Hold of the Data

Data is the lifeblood of AI; without it, AI is nothing. But data is all over the place, it is stored in different systems, in different silos, in different formats. Finding it, accessing it, cleaning it, and labeling it is time and resource intensive. Never underestimate the work and the risks involved here. Without good data, your AI project is going nowhere fast.

➜ Train the Model

Once you have the data, you use it to train models. This is also time consuming and can be expensive. But, it's worth the time and effort to do it properly. You will learn a lot in those early training days, including things you never expected to learn. If you came into AI thinking you could switch it on and walk away, you were wrong. Like a child, AI needs love, attention, and the time to learn before it is really effective. If you underestimate the work involved, you put your project at serious risk.

➜ Deploy to Production

Similarly, deploying models into production is a manual effort (currently) and needs to be planned for carefully to avoid bottlenecks. Again, you can't just switch something on and walk away. Everything from the features and the data to the model itself needs to be versioned, and different teams will likely need different features and versions of the same model. You need to manage all this deployment activity very carefully.

➜ Continuous Improvement

Once you have gone through the process of training your AI model, it's vital that you keep in mind that training data is different to the real-world messy data that the AI model will encounter once it is in production. What that means is that performance will almost certainly start to degrade right after deployment. Therefore, you need to proactively monitor that situation. Be ready for it, and ensure that you have monitoring alerts that tell you when any quality thresholds are breached. And of course, you need to ensure that production models are regularly re-trained over time.

→ Involve the Right People

There are lots of AI tools available, entire libraries full of them to draw upon, but the tools are worthless without the right people to use them. Probably the most important key to AI success is building the right team. Yes, you need some people that understand how to use the algorithms and manipulate the data, but just as importantly, you need people who understand your business, how it works, and how it can be improved. That's why you are using AI in the first place: to improve, to automate, to grow, not (just) because it's cool technology. Choose your team wisely, and build one that is lasting.

→ Select the Right AI Tools

The market place is crowded with often confusing and contradictory choices. The tools are still evolving; one tool may integrate well with your existing tech infrastructure, whilst another may not. AI can be magical, but it's not The Lord of the Rings—there is no one AI tool to rule them all. Some are good in one use case, others in another. Don't just buy something because you have seen it on TV or know the brand. Browse, consider, ask questions, and just like your team selection, choose wisely.

→ Transparency

Many AI developers naturally want to deliver the best and highest performance AI possible, but the highest performing AI is likely to be a black box that is not transparent or intuitive to humans and brings risks. Formal regulations may demand the explanation of an AI's predictions. Therefore, you must at least consider following so-called "human in the loop" best practices to supervise your AI, to ensure you can manage the risk of such challenges.

➡ Just Do It

AI technology is readily available, as is data. You don't need a PhD to get started; what you need is a reason. Find something in your organization that could be improved with the use of AI or ML, and get started. Go online and play with some AI tools today, listen and watch for what they do well and what they struggle with. Read articles, read some of the horror stories. You can learn a lot from how others did things wrong. Take our training course (we had to give it a plug)! Network with others in your organization or industry peer groups. Whatever you do, get started now. AI and ML are very powerful technologies that can bring great change, and they are more readily accessible than many think. However, you must always remember that (in the words of Joseph Beuys) "Truth must be found in reality, not systems." You run, control, and direct AI, not the other way round. You are in charge, and it's your time to step up. Carpe Diem!

➜ Next Steps

We hope you enjoyed this book and will use it in your day to day work in the world of AI. Alone it should provide you with valuable guidance on how to approach any enterprise AI project. However, you may want to learn more. There are many books and training courses available but most focus on AI technology itself rather than the practical considerations of implementing and using AI in the workplace.

Hence, biased though we may well be, we strongly recommend that you consider taking the training course we built and that inspired this book:

Practical AI for the Information Professional
www.aiim.org/ai

If you want more direct and hands on support and guidance, or even if you just want to ask questions of us, don't be shy, we can be easily contacted via email.

aps@deep-analysis.net
kashyap.kompella@rpa2ai.com

Good luck on your journey, and we look forward to hearing from you!

Printed in Poland
by Amazon Fulfillment
Poland Sp. z o.o., Wrocław

57442339R00085